THE SECRETS OF
ROSEMUNDY HOUSE

CLIVE BENNEY

The Secrets of Rosemundy House

FOREWORD

The writing of this book has been a labour of love for me over many years. I have known Rosemundy House for a long time and for several different reasons – dancing there at Flora Dances in the early 1960s, many wedding receptions attended there, including my own, and over the last eleven years I have given about 650 local history talks to guests staying at the hotel. The idea of writing the book was provided by the mothers I met who gave birth at the house during the time it was a Mother and Baby Home. I thought however that to do the house justice I would have to write its whole history from its building to the present day. This has proved quite a mammoth task, especially researching the many families that owned the house and lived there before it became the Mother and Baby Home in 1919. It soon became clear to me that this Georgian house, built around 1780, has a history to rival any television period drama. The problem that kept arising was that just when I thought I had all the information available, more arrived with wonderful photographs to accompany it – and how depleted the book would have been without some of these new treasures.

The largest portion of the book concerns the Mother and Baby Home, a place where pregnant girls, some as young as fourteen, were sent to have their babies. I have met and spoken to many of these mothers, and their stories are recorded in this book. Some mothers took their babies home with them, but so many, after just a few weeks, had to give them up for adoption. It is hard to imagine the heartache these mothers had to bear when they watched their lovely babies being taken away. Sadly, for so many mothers the stigma of Rosemundy Mother and Baby Home is still with them today. Some feel it simply for having given birth there, and others from the guilt that they gave their babies up for adoption, despite the fact that most had no choice. I hope this book might in some way help these mothers who have lived with the guilt for so long. They were not a small minority – about 1200 mothers gave birth there during the 45-year history of the Home. Just think how different things are today! For the children born there and given up for adoption the book might go some way to help them understand why their mothers had to do it.

To all mothers who gave birth at Rosemundy House

First published in 2014 by Wheal Hawke Publications:
14 Trevaunance Road, St Agnes, Cornwall, TR5 0SE
No part of this book may be reproduced without permission from the publisher
Design by Daniel Benney www.danielbenney.co.uk
ISBN 978-0-9550510-5-0
Printed by R Booth Ltd: The Praze, Penryn, Cornwall, TR10 8AA

The Secrets of Rosemundy House

CONTENTS

Portrait of the Reverend Isaac Donnithorne by Thomas Gainsborough R.A.
(Falmouth Art Gallery Collection).

THE DONNITHORNES AND DANIEL'S TENEMENT

For many years during the 18th century the land at St Agnes on which Rosemundy House was built was owned by the Donnithorne family. The Donnithornes were a Cornish family that ran Polberro Mine, one of the richest mines in Cornwall, producing profits of £100 a day and employing 250 workers. Nicholas Donnithorne was High Sheriff of Cornwall in 1731 and lived at Trevellas Manor near St Agnes. On his death all his assets were inherited by his eldest son Joseph. In 1762 Joseph died, and all land and property were then inherited by Joseph's younger brother, the Revd Isaac Donnithorne (1709-1782), who had been ordained an Anglican priest in 1735.

Prior to 1776, and before the building of Rosemundy House, the land on which it was later built was leased to a Mark Daniel by the Revd Isaac Donnithorne. It is not clear who Mark Daniel was, but it is known that at this time there was a Mark Daniell, victualler, living in St Agnes and another Mark Daniell, described in a lease as a gentleman.

In 1776 the land at Rosemundy was leased to John James. A covenant in the Carne Collection (Courtney Library, Royal Institution of Cornwall, Truro), dated 18th September 1776, from the Revd Isaac Donnithorne to John James Jnr. when he acquired the property, states that it was 'for holdin Rosemunday [sic] for 99 years if three lives shall so long live'. In this document the property is described as 'Messuage or dwelling house, mowhay, barn, stable, smiths shop, garden orchard and about one acre of land be the same more or less ... commonly called Rosemundy ... the antient dutchy [sic] of Cornwall, situate lying and being in the said Parish of St Agnes late in the possession of Mark Daniel ...'

This shows that prior to the building of Rosemundy House there was already a dwelling of some kind on the land occupied by Mark Daniel. The document continues:

> This indenture in the year one thousand seven hundred and seventy six between Isaac Donnithorne of Hereford ... of the one part and John James the younger of the Parish of St Agnes in the County of Cornwall, gentleman of the other part [unreadable] Isaac Donnithorne as well for and in consideration of the sum of two hundred pounds of lawful money ... yearly rent or sum of five shillings of lawful money of Great Britain.

The above covenant was on three lives, John James Jnr., Jacob James and James James.

JOHN JAMES

John James was from Mingoose, the son of James and Dinah James (née Fox). He acquired the lease on the property in 1776. It is believed that he built Rosemundy House shortly after this.

On the 23rd September 1777 he married Eleanor Harris from Truro, and the following year their first child, Mary Harris James, was born. On the 30th October 1779 a son, James (later known as the 'Little Lawyer'), was born; in 1781, Henry Harris James; in 1782, Dinah; in 1783, Eliza; in 1785, Harriot (a boy); in 1787, John; and in 1789, Robert.

In 1782 the Revd Isaac Donnithorne died, and the property was inherited by his son Nicholas, who continued the lease with John James.

John James was described in various documents as a mine purser, book keeper and mine manager. In the book *Friendly Retreat*, by Maurice Bizley, Stannary Court cases involving John James are mentioned. Included are:

> Case III. At the Court held in September, 1784, John James, of Rosemundy ..., Gentleman, as Purser, Book-keeper and Manager in Wh. Dellick claimed from Abraham Prout, of St. Agnes, who had adventured one-eighth part in the mine, the sum of £5. 8. 7¼ being his share of the cost of working the mine. The Court found for the Petitioner and also awarded £4. 10. 10 Costs against the Defendant.

Case VII. John James the Younger, of St. Agnes, Gent., as purser and manager of Turnavore Mine, petitioned against Richard Rouse, of Truro, Adventurer of 1/24th share in the mine, claiming £33. 18. 0 as his proportion for working the Mine.

The 1776 covenant was amended by Nicholas Donnithorne in 1785, with a new provision attached: 'that for any lives died within six years other lives could be added'. This new covenant further describes the property as '… more or less commonly called Rosemundy part of the mannor [sic] of Tywarnhayle and part parcel of the ancient Duchy of Cornwall'.

In the National Archives is a group of letters and papers dated March 1795. One letter is to the Home Office from General S. Hulse, enclosing information regarding the state of the County of Cornwall and stating that Mr Donnithorne is agent for the County and a gentleman of considerable property. Another letter is to General Hulse from Nicholas Donnithorne, following receipt of intelligence from Cornwall, urging immediate action to be taken 'to quiet the minds of the people, and that the East India Company be persuaded to ship 200 tons of tin to each of the markets of Bengal and Madras'.

The above letters seem to have resulted from a letter to Nicholas Donnithorne from John James, dated 20th March 1795, in which he described the shortage of bread corn in St Agnes parish. Rumours had reached the miners that a large quantity of corn was being shipped from Padstow. The plan of the principal inhabitants was to go and buy corn for the relief of the parish, but the miners refused to wait for this outcome and, together with miners from the south, assembled and set off on their own march on Padstow. The letter from John James (Rosemundy) continued:

> I am informed that Capt. Seymour, Captain Silvester, Jack Tregellas and my cousin at Rose in Vale [John James] set off this morning desiring the Tinners to quiet until their return, that they would do everything in their power to get corn brought into the Parish, however that was not sufficient to satisfy their minds and the aforesaid Gents had not been gone but a very short time before the whole Body moved after them. I shall wait till morning before I close this [letter].

The letter was continued on Saturday at 2 o'clock:

> It is reported that our miners got into St Columb yesterday afternoon about 4 o'clock that they behaved very well and the Town had made a very large subscription for them, to provide themselves refreshment and they left the Town in the greatest good order and arrived at Padstow about 9 o'clock, when they found 4 vessels loaded with Corn and the Cellars quite full, which they had taken possession of without by your leave or with your leave. It is now 6 o'clock no other news received.

In 1796 Nicholas Donnithorne died, leaving debts of £30,000. This seems strange as he had become heavily involved in the family mining business and in 1789 he worked alongside George Unwin to establish a contract to export Cornish tin to China. The East India Company accepted the scheme and 600 tons of coined tin was exported annually. Between 1791 and 1795 the trade amounted to roughly £400,000. In honour of the work of Nicholas Donnithorne and George Unwin, a tower paid for by public subscription was erected on St Agnes Beacon. The tower, crenellated and painted white, stood some 24 feet high and would have been a prominent landmark. Sadly, the tower was vandalised, and by the mid 19th century only rubble remained.

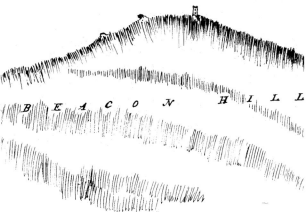

Left: Roger's Tower at Castle-an-Dinas c. 1910, believed to be similar to the one that stood on the Beacon.
Below: Sketch from plan of lands belonging to John James, 1814, showing the tower on the Beacon.

Nicholas Donnithorne
(St Agnes Museum Collection).

Nicholas died intestate, and Isaac, his eldest son, inherited the house and debts. To settle these debts, land and property had to be sold, and in 1797 a solicitor's letter was sent to Isaac Donnithorne concerning the sale of Rosemundy House and other property in the area. In this letter Isaac is advised to sell Rosemundy to John James, in these words:

> This estate can only be desirable to be possessed by Mr James, and to him must be an object of serious value. If he will pay a good price for it, it would be desirable to sell. N.B. On this piece of ground Mr James has erected an [sic] handsome dwelling house wherein he resides and other part converted into gardens.

The above document quite clearly tells us that John James built the 'handsome dwelling house', but what is not clear is whether this was a new house on the site or an extension of the earlier one mentioned in the covenant of 1776.

John James bought Rosemundy House and grounds and also a considerable amount of land in St Agnes, Penwinnick and Mingoose. He had also become a member of the Court Roll for the Manor of Tywarnhayle. In 1795 the court was held in his house at Rosemundy.

In 1811 John James acquired land from Thomas Olivie Prout. The lease, in the Carne Collection, refers to '... part of one field or close of land situate in the said Parish of St Agnes which lieth [sic] opposite to the Mansion House of Rosemundy ... Thomas Olivie Prout would retain the upper part of the field'.

John James had enough land to employ a gamekeeper, Richard Polglase, and in 1811 a game certificate was issued which covered 'Penwinnick and other lands'. He also employed an apprentice, but in October 1813 a small notice appeared in the *Royal Cornwall Gazette* under the heading 'Apprentice Absconded':

> George Philips Parish Apprentice to John James had run away and whoever harboured or employed him would be prosecuted. George was described as 'about 18 years of age, and about 5 feet 6 inches high'; he went off without any provocation whatever and carried away all his clothes.

It was believed that he might have been heading for a mine in Devon, since he had two brothers in that area.

Rosemundy House c. 1880, before the bay windows were added.

On 23rd March 1814 John James died, and the *West Briton* of the 25th March reported:

> At Rosemundy, on Wednesday morning, John James, Esq., aged 65, [died] after a long confinement, which he bore with exemplary resignation; he was a man of courteous manners and great affability, – humane, hospitable and benevolent, his friends and the poor will deeply regret their loss.

The following appeared in the *Royal Cornwall Gazette* of the 9th April 1814:

> All persons indebted to the estate of John James, late of Rosemundy, Esq. deceased are requested pay their respective debts into the CORNISH BANK, at Truro, to the account of William Sandys of Lanarth and Joseph Hoskin, of Ellenglase, Esquires, the Trustees and Executors named in the last Will and Testament. All persons having claims or demands upon the said estate are requested to make the same known to the said Trustees and Executors or to John James of Truro their solicitor.

The solicitor John James mentioned above lived at 'Rose in Vale' in Mithian and was a founder of Nalder's Solicitors in Truro. He was a cousin to John James (deceased) of Rosemundy House. It is quite noticeable how similar in design 'Rose in Vale' and Rosemundy House were before the major alterations over the years at Rosemundy.

On the 16th June 1914 the following notice appeared in the *Royal Cornwall Gazette* under the heading 'Delightful Residence and Fine Estate':

> To be sold, in one lot, by tender, ... all those valuable parts of land, late of the said John James, which are situate in and called Mingoose, Penwinnick, Bolster, Chengrouse, and Breannick; And the Dues of Mines on the waste of the same; Together with the Mansion-House, and Customary or Duchy Tenements of Rosemundy with the Plantations, Pleasure Grounds, Walled and other Gardens thereto belonging; all situate in the Parish of St Agnes, in the County of Cornwall, at a distance of eight miles from Truro; the Turnpike Road from which place passes through the Estates. The House consists of a good Dining Room, a Drawing Room, other Sitting Rooms, Ten Bedrooms, excellent Kitchen and Offices, and is delightfully situated in the midst of Gardens, Pleasure Grounds, and Rich Meadows, within five minutes walk of the Church

and Market Town of St Agnes and at a distance of about a mile from the Cove and Pier of Trevaunance; the whole is in perfect order of repair, and the possession of the same with the Farm House, and outbuildings of Penwinnick, and about 170 Acres of Land, now in hand, may be had at Michaelmas next; the other Parts of Lands are Let for Years or Lives ...

Further evidence to suggest that a building of some kind stood on the site prior to the building of Rosemundy House comes from an 1814 document held in the Carne Collection, which refers to the sale of Rosemundy House following the death of John James. It refers to 'The Mansion House, garden plantations, stable ... of Rosemundy formerly Daniel's Tenement ...'

Another document from this collection lists all the property John James owned and is entitled: *Particular of certain Customary and freehold and leasehold lands late of John James Esq. deceased situate in the parish of St Agnes in the County of Cornwall and conditions of sale of the same.* Together with Rosemundy House his property comprised:

At 'Mingoose' several cottages, Richards's stamping mill and a burning house. At 'Penwinnick' Penwinnick Farm, lawn and plantation opposite the house at Rosemundy, Mills tenement and Stickler's higher field. At 'Bolster', dwelling house and tenement, part of Goonvrea, house, garden and land. At 'Breannick', several properties including a large handsome new dwelling house, shop etc in the village of St Agnes, occupied by Edward Opie, mercer etc. Cleaderscroft plantation, Brother Tenement consisting of the Prince's Arms Inn with suitable out-houses, a small dwelling house adjoining, Shambles slaughter house etc.

In October 1815 the above land and properties appeared for sale in the *Royal Cornwall Gazette*. The sale consisted of 13 lots and again included Rosemundy House which at this time was occupied by Samuel Vincent Pryce, surgeon, as 'Tenant from year to year'. Little is known about this man except that he would later marry Sarah Coster Humphries, widow of Thomas Humphries, the next owner of Rosemundy House. (An 1833 deed concerning Wheal Leisure Copper Mine, held at the Cornwall Record Office, Truro (AD2064/16), includes the wording: 'Parties: 1) Samuel Vincent Pryce, surgeon of Redruth and Sarah Coster his wife, late Coster Humphries widow of Thomas Humphries, esquire, of Rosemundy ...').

In February 1816 another advertisement appeared in the newspaper for the sale of Rosemundy House, Penwinnick Farm and shares in various mines: West Wheal Kine Tin Mine, Wheal Harriet Tin Mine in St Agnes Parish and Wheal Deer Park lead and copper mine in Newlyn Parish. By July 1816 Rosemundy

House had still not sold, and another advertisement appeared in the paper, indicating that now the house was to be sold or let by private contract.

The house and farm still failed to sell, and in 1819 Rosemundy House and Penwinnick Farm came up for auction. The following appeared in the *West Briton* on the 9th and 16th July under the heading 'A Delightful Residence and Beautiful Farm':

> To be sold, in one or two lots, as may be agreed upon at the time of the sale, all that Capital Mansion House called ROSEMUNDY with the meadow and customary, or Duchy tenements, plantation and pleasure grounds, walled and other garden thereto belonging to the residence late of John James esq. deceased, situate in the Parish of St Agnes in the County of Cornwall.

The second lot was Penwinnick Farm with 59 acres, described as 'The fee-simple and inheritance of all that new-built dwelling house and beautiful farm called Penwinnick'. The auction was to be held at Pearce's Hotel in Truro on Monday the 2nd August at five o'clock in the afternoon. It would seem however that they still failed to sell because a similar advertisement appeared in the *West Briton* twelve months later, on the 28th July 1820.

Penwinnick Farm

THOMAS HUMPHRIES

By the early 1820s the house had been purchased by Thomas Humphries, a mine purser for various mines including Great St George, North Seal Hole and East Wheal Charlotte. Thomas lived at the house with his wife Sarah and their children. A description of the House at this time appears in the book *The history of Cornwall from the earliest records and traditions, to the present time* (1824):

> The only gentleman's seat in the parish is Rosemundy, lately the residence of John James deceased. The house is not large, but it is neat and convenient; and the grounds have lately been considerably improved.

Thomas died after a long illness on the 1st January 1831, aged just 50, and was buried in St Agnes churchyard.

Thomas Humphries'
headstone.

A notice dated 16th January 1831 appeared in the *Royal Cornwall Gazette* requesting that anyone having any claim to the estate of Thomas Humphries should contact Messrs Samuel or Henry Humphries at Rosemundy or Mr Turner, Truro Bank, Executors of the will.

Little more is known about Thomas except that just six months before his death he was involved in a High Court case against John Vivian and Charles Carpenter (defendants) regarding mining rights at the Great St George Copper Mine. The case was heard at Lincoln's Inn Hall before the Lord Chancellor.

HENRY HUMPHRIES

The house was inherited by Henry Humphries, Thomas' son; he was in his early twenties and, it appears, had no intention of retaining the property. On the 15th April 1831 it was advertised for sale in the *West Briton* under the heading 'Desirable and Delightful Family Residence, Rosemundy in St Agnes'. This time it was to be sold by private contract. The advertisement continued:

> All that Capital Mansion House and desirable family residence ROSEMUNDY, delightfully situated in the midst of gardens, pleasure-grounds, and rich meadows between three and four acres.

The notice then lists the rooms and their dimensions and advises of the 'Excellent Quarry on the premises'. For a view of the premises and other particulars the reader was asked 'to apply to Mr Humphries at Rosemundy'.

A month later, on the 20th May, the *West Briton* advertised the auction sale of the furniture and effects at Rosemundy, which included 'Splendid modern furniture, comprising Rosewood and mahogany tables and chairs, Pier and Chimney glasses, maps etc.' The auction was to take place on the '24th May and the following days at 11 o'clock in the forenoon, of each day, until the whole are disposed of, at Rosemundy House in the Parish of St Agnes the late residence of Thomas Humphries, esq. deceased'.

Henry like his father was a mine purser and in April 1831 advertised in the *Royal Cornwall Gazette* for a good, second-hand engine, forty to forty-five inch cylinder.

In March 1832 farm stock was auctioned at Penwinnick, the property of the late Thomas Humphries. This included nine very valuable cart horses, two excellent cows and calves, two prime fat oxen, one fat bull, two ewes and lambs etc.

In May 1832 Henry married Mary Anne Sleeman from Truro.

Rosemundy House was again advertised for sale or let in August 1832. The house was described as 'a very desirable residence for the Genteel Family'.

In October 1832 Rosemundy was broken into while the family were out, and a quantity of cash was stolen. Suspicion fell on a family living nearby. The offenders were apprehended and on the 30th March 1833 the *Royal Cornwall Gazette* carried the following report:

> At the Cornwall Lent Assizes at Launceston John Butson and Elizabeth Butson were indicted for breaking into the dwelling house of Mr Henry Humphries, at St Agnes, and stealing therefrom 21 sovereigns and 17 five-pound notes; Joanna Butson was indicted for receiving the property, knowing it to be stolen. Mr Humphries stated that he is a purser and superintendent of some mines near St Agnes where he lives. The prisoners live within 100 yards of his house. On Friday the 5th October last he and Mrs Humphries went from home leaving two servant maids in charge of the house in which he left in a secretary 21 sovereigns, two or three pounds in silver, chiefly in half crowns and £135 in Truro five-pound banknotes; the remainder was in checks [sic]. On the Sunday after, whilst the servants were at Church, the house was entered; the secretary was broken open and the sovereigns, banknotes and silver were carried off. Suspicion fell on the prisoners whose house was searched and concealed in it was a chisel that corresponded to the marks made in forcing the secretary from whence the property was taken; two sheets, a pair of gloves and other articles were found concealed in the house of the prisoners. The chisel was admitted by the male prisoner as belonging to him; several sovereigns were found on Joanna Butson the mother of the other two prisoners, and she dropped several expressions when taken into custody which left no doubt as to the guilt of her son and herself.
> The jury found the son and mother "guilty" and acquitted the daughter. John Butson, sentence of death, recorded. Joanna Butson to be imprisoned for two years.

In *An account of St Agnes life by Isaac Rowse (1822-1908) as he knew and remembered it,* held at St Agnes Museum, the author states:

> Apart from drunkenness and misdemeanours associated with it, there is only one record of serious crime reported in these years, and that was a robbery at Rosemundy House in about 1835.

> The house was occupied by a Mr Humphreys [sic] and one Sunday while the residents were at church, the house was broken into by two brothers and a sister called Butson. They were discovered and caught, and at their trial at Bodmin the two men were sent to Botany Bay, the woman being told by the judge, 'But for your grey hair you would have accompanied your brothers'. Instead she was imprisoned in Bodmin Gaol.

Quite clearly these two incidents are the same, the second account having been distorted slightly owing to the passage of time. It does however seem likely that the death sentence on John Butson, reported in the newspaper, was not carried out and that he was transported to Botany Bay.

On the 20th April 1833 the following advertisement appeared in the *Royal Cornwall Gazette*:

> To be sold by auction by Mr John Tippett on Wednesday the 15th May next at four in the afternoon at Mr Pearce's Hotel in Truro all that Capital House called ROSEMUNDY in St Agnes. Very delightfully situated in the midst of gardens, pleasure grounds and rich meadows, containing approximately four acres.

> The House, which is in good repair, consists of an excellent Dining-room 22 feet by 17; Drawing-room 18 feet by 15; Breakfast-parlour 14 feet by 10; best Bed-room 16 feet by 15; Middle Ditto 15 feet by 9; End-room 13 feet by 9; Dressing Ditto 21 feet by 15; Bed-room 17 feet by 15; ditto 17 feet by 11; ditto 15 feet by 10; with excellent Kichens, Offices, Pantries and Water-closet. Also cellar, coach house, four stalled stable and a commodious yard. The above is Duchy land in which is an excellent quarry. It is within five minute walk of the Church and market town of St Agnes and about half a mile from the romantic port of Trevaunance and eight miles from Truro ... The house and grounds may be viewed on application to Mr Humphries.

Although wanting to sell Rosemundy House, Henry was involved in the social life of the village. In July 1833, together with Lieut. Snowe, R.N., he acted as a steward at the St Agnes boat race regatta, as the *Royal Cornwall Gazette* of the 20th July reported:

> ... the romantic scenery and high cliffs contiguous to the cove of Trevaunance was greatly enlivened by the number of spectators (supposed to be from two to three thousand) witnessing the races, which was [sic] confined to fishing boats of two classes belonging to St Agnes, Perran Porth [sic] Newquay, Porthtowan and Portreath ...

The court case of 1830 involving Thomas Humphries continued to 1836, with Henry now becoming involved. The following appeared in the *West Briton* under the Cornwall Lent Assizes, concerning a case of 'Vivian and others vs. Humphries and others':

> The defendants were Henry Humphries of Rosemundy, the managing agent of Great St George Copper mine situate in the several parishes of St Agnes and Perranzabuloe ... Mr Vivian claimed the mining rights under a sett from Mr Carpenter the Duchy lessee, dated the 18th day of May 1830, ... [and] the defendants claimed the mining rights under a sett from the same party, dated the 11th day of September, 1822 – which was granted to John Williams, Esq. of Scorrier House, and the late Capt. Thos. Trelease of Perranzabuloe, who assigned the same to the late Thomas Humphries, Esq., the father of one of the defendants ...

After a short consultation the jury found the case for the defendants.

Wednesday 5th July 1837 was a general holiday in St Agnes to celebrate the accession of Queen Victoria to the throne. By 3 o'clock thousands of people had assembled in Churchtown and Henry Humphries read the proclamation. At the end of the ceremony he gave an address to the spectators, which was received with a loud cheer.

Rosemundy was still for sale on the 18th January 1839, when the following appeared in the *West Briton* under 'St Agnes':

> We understand that the Dean and Chapter of Exeter have recently purchased the neat and commodious residence of Rosemundy, in this parish, to be occupied as the vicarage-house, and that the Rev. Canon Rogers manifestly contributed just the half of the sum required for the

Churchtown in the mid 1800s (note the cobbled street, removed around 1850).

purpose. It is understood that the Chapter are also looking for a suitable premises in Perran, for a similar object, and that when these and some other contemplated arrangements are completed, there will be a resident vicar in each parish.

The following however appeared in the same paper on the 8th February:

We are informed that the statement made in the paper a fortnight since respecting the purchase of Rosemundy for the residence of the vicar of this parish was premature. A negotiation had been entered on between the Rev Canon Rogers on the part of the Dean and Chapter and the proprietor. Our Correspondent heard that the bargain had been completed, the sum given or to have been given was even mentioned to him. It turns out however that the requisite funds cannot be calculated on with sufficient certainty to justify the Canon in proceeding further at present.

Mr Humphries still owned the property in 1839 when the *West Briton* of the 7th June, under 'Blackwater', reported:

A Bible Association was formed in the village on Thursday the 30th ult. [i.e. May]. H. Humphries esq. of Rosemundy was in the chair. The meeting was addressed by the Chairman, the Revs J. Whitworth, J. Thomas, B. Woodyard and H. Whitworth Esq., surgeon of St Agnes ...

(The H. Whitworth, surgeon of St Agnes, mentioned above, was Henry Whitworth, the first of a long line of Whitworths who became doctors in St Agnes. 1839 was the year when he first came to the village. The Rev. James Whitworth was his father and a Methodist Minister in the Redruth circuit.)

By the 1841 census Henry Humphries had eventually sold Rosemundy House and moved with his family to Bristol. He is shown living with his wife Mary and three children: Emily, Charlotte and Sarah, all of whom had been born at Rosemundy House. Henry became a corn merchant and continued this occupation until just before his death in January 1883.

WILLIAM CARNE

In the 1841 census William Carne is shown as living at Rosemundy House and had obviously acquired the property around 1840. He was a wine and spirit merchant and ship owner from Falmouth, and with his brother, Edward Clifton Carne, ran the business W. and E.C. Carne. William was 45 years old in 1841 and lived at the house with his wife Mary, also 45, and their servant Emma Smith, aged 20.

In her book *Old Falmouth* (published 1903) Susan E. Gay wrote:

> The Carnes, an old family of Welsh origin, have been connected with Falmouth for more than a hundred and fifty years. As shippers and importers, as well as bankers and wine and general merchants (including timber, etc.), and manufacturers, they possessed an important business. They acquired the Falmouth branch of the business of John Camin, of London, through the marriage of Mr. Richard Carne to a niece of the former in 1757.

In July 1846 William donated £5 to the fund for victims of the East Wheal Rose mine disaster. The mine was near St Newlyn East. The morning of the 9th July was bright and sunny, but just before mid-day clouds began to form, and lightning and thunder were followed by torrential rain concentrated on that area. Water flowed down the hills in torrents, and despite efforts by men at the surface to dam or divert the water from the shafts the mine was rapidly flooded up to the 50 fathom (300 ft) level. Thirty-nine miners were drowned.

William was still living at Rosemundy House in 1848 when the *West Briton* of the 5th May reported on the death of John Penberthy, aged 31, who died when he fell down the shaft of Polbreen Mine looking for the gates that had previously been stolen from 'Mr Carne of Rosemundy'.

In 1846 St Agnes gained its independence from Perranzabuloe and became a separate ecclesiastical parish. The Revd Alexander Allen Vawdrey was appointed first vicar of St Agnes on the 1st May. The church building at this time was in a poor state of repair. It dated from the 15th century and had become filled with timber required to prop it up. In addition, four of the arches had been removed, one to give a former churchwarden a better view of the officiating clergyman from his pew. The roof had begun to fall in and the walls consequently to fall out. The new vicar made restoration a priority and with the help of William Carne set about raising funds for the project. In August 1848 the cornerstone of the new building was laid. The weather being fine, a large number of people attended the event, and following this the clergy and other visitors, about a hundred in all, were entertained by William in the grounds of Rosemundy House. Two long tables and a cross-table at the head were arranged on the lawn under a tent formed with flags and decorated with evergreens and flowers.

The building of the church continued under the direction of Mr J. Piers St Aubyn, architect, with William and his wife taking a leading part in the restoration. The east window became a memorial to them.

In April 1849 Rosemundy House appears in the *Royal Cornwall Gazette* for sale or rent. The advertisement describes the property as

> Consisting of Dining, Drawing and Breakfast-rooms, Library, seven Bed-rooms, including servants', two Dressing-rooms, Butler's Pantry, an excellent Kitchen, Dairy, and every requisite for a Gentleman's family. Also a Stable, Coach-House and Cow-house. It is eight miles from Truro, seven from Redruth, and about a quarter of a mile from the sea, is prettily situated and in most complete order; it has a good garden, well stocked with young trees of the choicest fruits ...

By July 1849 the building of the new Parish Church was completed and the official opening took place. The church was full and after the service many visitors remained, admiring the structure. They then adjourned to Rosemundy House and 160 people had refreshments on the lawn under a tent formed of flags. The Revd W.J. Cope proposed the health of their kind host, Mr Carne, as the active promoter of the good work whose completion they had met to celebrate.

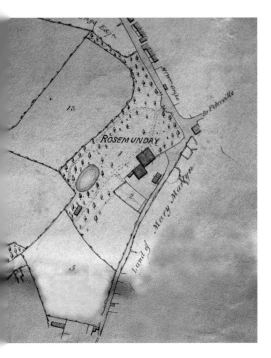

Rosemundy House and grounds in 1840.

A portrait of William Carne painted by Sidney Hodges.

Mr Carne briefly and feelingly expressed his sympathy with the parish in which he had lived for ten years, and which he was now about to leave, and proposed a toast to 'St Agnes and its parishioners'.

By 1851 William had moved back to Falmouth, and the census shows him living in Market Street with his wife Mary and two servants.

William was to become the Mayor of Falmouth in 1855 and again in 1863 and 1864. In 1865 the inhabitants of Falmouth commissioned Mr Sidney Hodges to paint a portrait of him. The inscription read 'William Carne, Mayor, 1855, 1863, 1864. Presented by his fellow-townsmen, 1865'.

In *Old Falmouth* (1903) the Carne family were described as being

> ... engaged in many of its public affairs, charitable and otherwise, among them, in later years, the making of the railway to Falmouth, with which Mr. William Carne had much to do; he was in fact chairman of the Cornish line, although by some irony of fate when it came it cut right across the sweet garden of the "Cottage," his own home.

The St Agnes census of 1851 states 'Rosemundy uninhabited', but the property still remained in the ownership of the Carne family.

GEORGE HUGOE

In May 1850 a newspaper advertisement appeared, offering Penwinnick Farm, also owned by William Carne, for rent. It was described as a desirable estate consisting of about 57 acres of land with dwelling house etc. To view the estate, people were asked to apply to Mr George Hugoe, who lived on the property. Rent would be received by Mr Carne. In September all the animals at Penwinnick were auctioned, and again interested people were asked to apply to Mr Hugoe.

It would appear that George Hugoe was employed by the Carne family and lived at Penwinnick, but later, presumably after the farm had been let and William had moved back to Falmouth, Mr Hugoe moved into Rosemundy House. He was certainly living there in June 1855 when an advertisement for guano manure appeared in the newspaper. It had been imported direct from Peru, and interested persons were asked to apply to William Carne at Falmouth or Mr Geo. Hugoe at Rosemundy, St Agnes.

In the 1861 census George Hugoe, aged 40, is still living at Rosemundy House with his wife Emma, aged 35, his father Thomas, aged 73, and Jane Tippett as servant. George's occupation is given as a 'wine merchant's clerk'.

By the 1871 census George Hugoe had left Rosemundy and was living with his family at Coosebean.

WILLIAM NAYLOR CARNE

By the mid-1860s Rosemundy was occupied by William Naylor Carne. He was the son of Charles Frederick Carne, a brother to William Carne, who had lived at Rosemundy House from about 1840 to 1850. William Naylor Carne was born in Liverpool in 1840, and although not a Cornishman by birth, his ancestors had always lived in or near Falmouth. In the 1861 census he is shown living in Lancashire, aged 21, and his occupation is listed as Clerk to a General Banker. In *Old Falmouth* we read:

> A portrait of Richard Carne and his wife, Mr. and Mrs. Camin and other members of the family, hang on the walls of Mr. William Naylor Carne's beautiful residence, Rosemundy, (inherited from his uncle), at St. Agnes, among other family legacies.

William Naylor Carne married Catherine Charlotte Groube in 1863, and their son George was born at Kenwyn, Truro, in July 1864. Since their second son Frederick was born at Rosemundy in June 1865, it appears that the family moved to Rosemundy between these dates.

In 1865 William Naylor joined the family business of W. and E.C. Carne, working with his uncle William and cousin Edward Clifton Carne. William Carne died in 1869, leaving the business to be run by the two cousins.

Clockwise from top left: William Naylor Carne when he first arrived at Rosemundy.

The Carne Brewery in Falmouth, now Marks and Spence[...]

Edith, George, Alfred, Frederick and Arthur Carne outsic[...] the front door of Rosemundy House.

In the 1871 census William Naylor Carne, aged 31, is shown as a Wine Merchant, Rope Manufacturer, Miller, Maltster, Brewer, Manufacturer of Aerated Water, Ship Broker and Land Owner, employing five Maltsters and two boys, three Millers and two boys, four Clerks and one boy, seven Ale Bottlers and three boys, one woman and two girls and Porters. He is living at Rosemundy with his wife Catherine, aged 28, and four children: George, aged 6 (born at Kenwyn), Frederick, aged 5, Alfred, aged 3, and Edith, aged 2 (all born at St Agnes). On the 23rd August 1872 a fourth son, Arthur Camin, was born to William and Catherine.

A path ran through the grounds of Rosemundy House and came out opposite Lawrence Villas in Goonown. Mr Carne allowed the Goonown Chapel to use this path through his grounds for tea treats. The *Royal Cornwall Gazette* of the 19th July 1873 reported:

> Goonown Wesleyan Sunday School had its annual tea treat on Saturday last. The teachers and scholars, numbering about 700, met in the afternoon and forming a procession, headed by Camborne Rifle Corps Band marched through the grounds of Mr Carne, Rosemundy, and eventually to a field, where they had tea and several games were indulged in.

Like his uncle, William Naylor became involved in village life and in 1873 was appointed Chairman of the new St Agnes Burial Board. In the early nineteenth century the population of St Agnes had grown rapidly, Cornish tin was in great demand and mining was a thriving activity. Miners flooded in to St Agnes as one of the centres of this mining boom. The burial ground in the centre of the village was nearing its capacity and the churchyard attached to the parish church was relatively small. The diocese decided that the only solution to the problem was to purchase an additional piece of land. Penwinnick was selected for the new site.

In September 1877 a bazaar was held at Rosemundy House to raise funds to build a Church Sunday School. The school was very much needed – the *Royal Cornwall Gazette* reported 'The children at present meeting twice every Sunday in the church, and causing great inconvenience to the congregation by the removal of their books'. Mr Carne granted the use of his storeroom and the place was tastefully decorated with flags, flowers and evergreens. £52 was raised.

In 1878 another daughter, Charlotte Mary, was born to William and Catherine. To help look after the younger children Lucy Oxland was employed by the Carnes as a governess.

Rear l-r: Harry Oxland, William Naylor Carne, Lucy Carne (née Oxland), ?; *middle:* Con Oxland, ?; *front:* Granny Oxland (née Elizabeth Pascoe), Mr and Mrs Pascoe, Mary Oxland with her daughter Mary on her lap.

On the 15th November that year, however, great sadness came to Rosemundy House when William's wife Catherine died, leaving him with six young children.

In January 1880 William married Lucy Oxland, his children's governess, in Plymouth. She was the sister of the Revd Harry Oxland, from Illogan. In the 1881 census for Rosemundy House, William Naylor Carne is shown aged 41, a shipping agent and wine merchant, with his new wife, Lucy, aged 26, and children Edith, aged 12, Arthur, aged 8 and Charlotte, aged 3. He employed a cook, parlourmaid, housemaid and nurse.

On the 16th April 1881 a daughter, Lucy Muriel (known as Muriel) was born to William and Lucy.

In December 1882 William Naylor Carne and his wife gave a magic lantern and musical entertainment in the Oddfellows Hall, Vicarage Road (now the Meadery). The magic lantern show included views of ruined abbeys and cathedrals, and marine views.

On the 9th December 1883 a second daughter, Gladys Naylor, was born to William and Lucy.

In 1886 William's cousin Edward Clifton died, and William became the sole owner of the family business.

In April 1887 William advertised in the *Royal Cornwall Gazette* for staff at Rosemundy House. He wanted a good plain cook (dairy and baking), a thorough house-parlour maid and a laundry maid, ages not under 30. In December the post of good plain cook was re-advertised, offering 'liberal wages to competent person'.

About 1890 William carried out major alterations to the house. He removed the original staircase, extended the building and added the bay windows.

In the 1891 census William Naylor Carne is shown at Rosemundy with his wife Lucy and children Charlotte Mary, aged 13, Lucy Muriel, aged 9, Gladys Naylor, aged 7 and his mother-in-law Elizabeth Oxland. A school governess, cook, domestic servant and housemaid were also shown. The census further

Rosemundy House with bay windows added (c. 1900).

indicates another property at Rosemundy where the gardener lived. This was Harry Williams, aged 66, who lived there with his wife Mary Ann, daughter Mary G. and grandson Henry. This additional property appears to be a single-storey dwelling that stood in the grounds to the left of the main entrance. Later, in his will, William Naylor Carne describes it as '... my adjoining dwelling house known as the Bungallow'.

On the 30th March 1891 William's eldest daughter Edith married James Thomas Farrant in Punjab, India, and on the 11th November that year his son Frederick William married Lucy Isabella Farrant, a sister of Thomas Farrant.

At the end of August 1894 a distinguished group of people came to Rosemundy House. The new P. and O. ship 'Caledonia' arrived off Cornwall and passengers were brought to Malpas by the 'S.S. Princess May' and to Truro by carriages. The *Royal Cornwall Gazette* reported:

> A group of 30 guests including Sir Owen and Lady Burne, Messrs Moberly Bell, of the Times; Henry Lucy, 'Toby' of Punch; Frank Burnand, editor of Punch; the Right Hon. Sir F. Jeune, president of the Admiralty Court; the Hon. Miss Davey, daughter of Lord Davey; Sir Thomas Sutherland, K.C.M.C. M.P. chairman of the P. and O. Company; Mr Steward Gladstone, director P. and O. Co. and the Bank of England; Lady Vaux, wife of Lord Vaux, of Harroden; Mr Macdonald, of Millend; Mons. Charles de Lesseps, of the Suez Canal; Messrs. Levvin Hill, of the Post-Office; Raymond Blathwayt, Austin Chamberlain, M.P., and Aird, M.P. drove to Perranporth and thence to Rosemundy, St Agnes, the residence of Mr. W.N. Carne of the firm W. and E.C. Carne, the oldest agents of P. and O. Co., where they were entertained to luncheon ...

In August 1895 notice was given in the Parish Church that Arthur Fleming Carne, son of William Naylor, intended to offer himself for Holy Orders.

In the mid-1890s William Vivian Smale became the gardener at Rosemundy House. Previously he had been an innkeeper at Calstock, had strawberry fields and grew soft fruits. In August 1896 his wife gave birth to a son, also named William Vivian Smale, at Rosemundy. On the birth certificate the father is shown as a gardener/domestic servant at Rosemundy House.

In 1897 more tragedy hit William when his son Alfred Wilmot was killed in South Africa.

Lucy with daughters Gladys and Muriel outside Rosemundy House.

Rear l-r: ?, Harold Twite, James Thomas Farrant, Lucy Carne, William Naylor Carne, Reg. Twite; *middle:* Lucy Isabella Carne (née Farrant), Gladys Naylor Carne, Charlotte Mary Carne, Lucy Muriel Carne, Edith Farrant (née Carne), Frederick William Carne; *front:* Evelyn Mary Farrant (Dolly), Charles Henry Carne, ?, Lucy Carne Farrant, Edwin Frederick Carne.

Lucy riding her tricycle with daugher Gladys on the back.

William's daughters Lucy Muriel and Gladys became excellent musicians on
the piano and violin – Gladys was playing before audiences in Germany at the
age of 10. Rosemundy House would have been full of musical sounds as the
girls grew up. Their mother's family, the Oxlands, were very musical.
Both daughters attended the Royal Academy of Music in London, and the
Royal Cornwall Gazette of the 28th July 1898 reported:

> At the distribution of honours to the students of the Royal Academy of
> Music in the Queens Hall, London, by H.R.H. the Duchess of York, on
> Friday last, Miss Lucy Muriel Carne and Miss Gladys Naylor Carne,
> daughters of Mr Naylor Carne of Rosemundy, St Agnes, Cornwall,
> received two medals each, one for piano and the other for violin.

Muriel and Gladys holding their violins.

Gladys and Muriel wearing their Royal Academy medals.

More awards followed in July 1899, leading to a further report in the *Royal Cornwall Gazette*:

> At the annual Royal Academy of Music prize distribution at the Queen's Hall, London, on the 21st July by the Countess of Radnor, Lucy Muriel Carne and Gladys Naylor Carne of Rosemundy, St Agnes, Cornwall received two silver medals each for piano and violin playing, the latter being awarded in addition a bronze medal for sight singing.

In April 1900 William, now the churchwarden, announced that he was prepared to build a new vestry at his own expense and to present it, together with an additional piece of land, to the church, in memory of his son, who had died in South Africa. The vicar, the Revd Alfred Rudall, characterised Mr Carne's offer as a noble one.

Yet more awards came to Lucy and Gladys in July 1900. The *Royal Cornwall Gazette* of the 2nd August reported:

> Sir Henry Irving distributed the annual awards of the Royal Academy of Music at the Queens Hall, London, on the 25th ult. [i.e. July], when the misses Lucy Muriel and Gladys Naylor Carne, daughters of W. Naylor Carne, of Rosemundy, St Agnes each received certificates (the highest award for the academy) for both piano and violin, the former also winning a bronze and the latter a silver medal for sight singing.

On the 2nd February 1903 Gladys made her debut at St James's Hall, London. She essayed Tchaikovsky's First Piano Concerto and Bruch's G Minor Violin Concerto in one concert. Later that year, on the 15th September, she played at the BBC Promenade Concert, in the Queen's Hall, London. The first Proms Concert had taken place here on the 10th August 1895 in the newly built hall. She played Camille Saint-Saëns' Concerto for Piano no. 2 in G minor, op. 22. Henry Wood was the conductor with the Queen's Hall Orchestra.

William was very proud of his house and gardens and much time was spent tending them. In December 1901, Mr. C. Ilott, lecturer to the County Council, gave a lecture in the garden on 'Fruit Culture and Management of Vegetable Gardens'. In April the following year he gave another talk on asparagus growing.

The following passage appears in *Old Falmouth*:

> Mr. Carne is one of the Cornish "gardeners," and his green-houses hold rare ferns and plants, while in his garden are to be seen fine shrubs and flowers, well sheltered by large trees.

In the December 1905 edition of the book *The Cornish Riviera*, issued by the Great Western Railway (originally in 1903), the following is written about the gardens:

> ... in the delightful garden of Mr. Naylor Carne, a pioneer of the cultivation of narcissi in endless variety, the luxuriance of tropical plants like the giant palm ... proves that although we are on the northern coast of Cornwall, the latitude is still that of "Troy Town" [Fowey].

Greenhouse

'... fine shrubs and flowers, well sheltered by large trees'

Summerhouse

Croquet lawn

Above: Entrance and Rosemundy Hill c. 1890.
Below: Entrance c. 1900.

On the 2nd February 1905 the *Royal Cornwall Gazette* carried the following report:

> The demolition of some old houses in what is locally known as Piccadilly Square is preparatory to the erection of a new vestry and caretaker's house for the Parish Council by W.N. Carne in memory of his son who died in South Africa.

William Naylor Carne also owned much property in Falmouth, as described in *Old Falmouth*:

> Mr. Naylor Carne, the present head of the family in Cornwall, has spared no expense in making certain of his buildings in the town picturesque or ornamental, within or without, according to their style, thereby improving the appearance of the Market Strand and the old street. He is also the owner of some old places in the town, Bell's Court, Mulberry Square, the Well, and property in High Street belonging to the late Mr. Jeffery. The "Cottage," with its rose-covered front, built when the adjacent road was a winding lane amid flowering hedge-rows, is still in his possession as owner, and remains unaltered.

Rear entrance showing courtyard and stabling c. 1900.

Although living at St Agnes, William's life was chiefly associated with Falmouth and Truro. As well as running his business, W. and E.C. Carne, he was a valued member of Falmouth Chamber of Commerce and became chairman of that body. He was president of the Philharmonic Society; chairman of Messrs Furniss and Company, biscuit manufacturers, Truro; a director of the Falmouth Gas Company; and chairman of the Truro Exchange Building Company. He took a keen interest in horticultural pursuits and was a judge at local shows.

On the 13th October 1906 William died, aged 67 years. The *West Briton* of the 4th October carried a long article:

> There passed away on Sunday, at St Agnes, one of the most prominent and highly-respected business men in Cornwall in the person of Mr. William Naylor Carne, sole proprietor of the firm Messrs. W. and E.C. Carne, of Falmouth and Truro. The deceased gentleman had been in ill health for some considerable time, although it was generally thought that he was making fair progress towards complete recovery ... Although not a Cornish-man by birth, Mr Carne had been associated with Cornish interests for practically the whole of his life ... The funeral, which was one of the largest seen in the parish for many years, took place at St Agnes yesterday morning, and the aspect of gloom which the little village wore, the crowded congregation at the Parish Church, and the expression of sorrow clearly visible on all the faces, were testimonies to the regret felt at the loss of a much respected inhabitant ...

In 1907 William's daughter Lucy Muriel Carne (Muriel) married Harold Llewellyn Twite, a mining engineer. He was the second son of Charles and Anna Twite of Castle House, St Agnes. Harold (known as Wellyn, after his second name) was educated at home and then at the Royal School of Mines in London.

In 1911, at the age of 32, Wellyn and a partner set up their own mining consultancy (Twite & Stannard) at 65 London Wall, and in 1912 he was contracted by the owners to manage the setting up of the world's largest wolfram mine, at Mawchi in northern Burma (Myanmar). Tungsten was at that time in great demand throughout the world for light bulbs and in particular for armour plating. He returned to London at least twice over the next year or so, to report in person to the shareholders. During this time Muriel was left in their house in Sutton with a maid, a nanny and a governess to help her with the children. In 1913 she accompanied

Above: Castle House, Trevaunance Road c.1900.

her husband on his return to Burma, leaving her three children, Charles (5), Barbara (4) and Betty (15 months) with the nanny and governess. She remained away for a period of about 15 months.

At the outbreak of World War I in 1914 Wellyn and Muriel had serious worries about the children, fearing that England might be invaded at any time. In September 1914 they boarded the 'S.S. Derbyshire' in Rangoon, bound for Southampton.

Back in England, Wellyn was commissioned as a lieutenant into the Royal Field Artillery and posted for training to Dover, Aldershot and other centres in the south-east. After months of requesting, he eventually managed to get himself seconded to the 183rd (Tunnelling) Company of the Royal Engineers in order to enable him to use his expertise to help with trench warfare. He was shipped to France in September 1915, and once at the front he led a team of Cornish miners (some from St Agnes) in sinking shafts and tunnelling in a race to detonate large explosions under the German trenches before they could retaliate.

On Wednesday the 1st December 1915, having that afternoon set off a mine under the German trenches, he and four of his fellow Cornishmen had just climbed back up the shaft to surface and were recording notes in the 'shaft

Harold Llewellyn Twite in his Royal Engineers' uniform.

office dug-out', a large earth cavern under a heavy soil roof, when at 8pm the enemy detonated a huge mine nearby. This caused the roof of the 'office' to collapse, burying all five men under tonnes of earth and rubble. By the time they were dug out some minutes later, they were all dead.

His widow Muriel commissioned a brass plaque on the north wall of the nave of St Agnes Church to commemorate him and the nine of his fellow Cornish miners from his company who were killed in action.

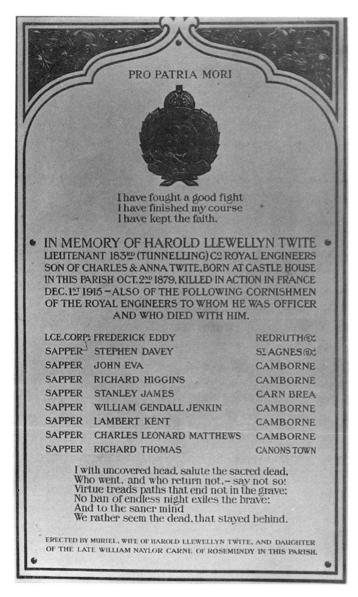

Brass plaque in St Agnes Church.

Lucy Carne remained at Rosemundy House and by 1908 the new vestry, planned by William, had been built. In April that year it was used for the first time. The *Royal Cornwall Gazette* of the 30th April reported on the meeting:

> Held for the first time in the new vestry built by the late Mr William Naylor Carne (dedicated after his death) in memory of his son, Alfred Wilmot Carne, who died in South Africa in 1897. Those present gratefully remembered the kindness of the donor and his love for all Church work.

On the 25th February 1909 the same newspaper recorded that 'Mrs Naylor Carne has given a very valuable set of altar clothes to the Parish Church'. She also presented the church with a brass Angel Lectern in memory of her husband, who had regularly read the lesson there.

In 1909 Rosemundy House was sold: on the 25th, 26th, 27th and 30th March the contents of the house were auctioned. The auction catalogue cover listed the various items for sale and the days on which the contents of each room would be sold.

Cover of auction catalogue.

George Carne and his family at Garras. *Standing (l-r):* George, Tremona, James, Daphne, Ruth; *seated:* William, Annie, George Snr.

Following William's death the family business of W. and E.C. Carne was taken over by George Newby Carne, William's eldest son. George had married Annie Emily Le Poer Power in 1897 and moved to Falmouth to live. In 1909 George commissioned an architect to build a new family home in Falmouth. This was built on the corner of Western Terrace and Pennance Road and was called Garras (later the Greenlawns Hotel and today Merchants Manor). George and Annie had six children: William Power, Jessie Tremona (Monie), Daphne Naylor, Harriett Ruth, James Power and George Power. All three sons had distinguished military careers. William served in the Royal Navy, seeing combat in both World Wars, and retired as Commodore (CBE). James joined the Gloucestershire Regiment and was awarded the Victoria Cross for courage. Lieutenant Colonel (later Colonel) Carne was commanding officer of the 1st Battalion of the Gloucestershire Regiment in the Korean War. On the 22nd/23rd April 1951 near the Imjin River, his battalion was heavily engaged by vastly superior numbers of the enemy. Throughout this time he moved among the whole battalion under heavy mortar and machine-gun fire, inspiring the utmost confidence and the will to resist among the troops. He personally led assault parties which drove the enemy back and saved important situations. George became a Major in the Army, serving with distinction in the Burma campaign, and was awarded the Military Cross.

Colonel James Power Carne V.C., D.S.O.

ROWE & KNOWLES

STRAND, FALMOUTH (TEL.: 189 & 1308).

By direction of the Executors of G. N. Carne, Esq., deceased.

CORNISH RIVIERA

GARRAS, FALMOUTH.

Substantially Built Freehold Residence of distinctive charm facing sea.

Vacant Possession.

Main services. Hall, 3 reception, 10 bed and dressing rooms, 2 bathrooms; nursery suite of 2 rooms; ample domestic offices.

Architect designed.

1¼ ACRES or thereabouts of well maintained and delightful grounds.

AUCTION—Falmouth, January 19th, 1955 (unless sold privately).

The sale of Garras in 1955.

FRANCIS NEWBERY ADKIN

Rosemundy House was purchased by Francis Newbery Adkin, a retired tobacco manufacturer from Bromley, Kent. He was married to Elizabeth Jewell Adkin (née Whitmore). The family however did not move into the house immediately, as the 1911 census lists its occupant as Thomas Collins, a caretaker/carpenter born in Bromley. Mr and Mrs Adkin are still shown as living at Westwood, Oaklands Road, Bromley.

Thursday 22nd June 1911 was Coronation Day and every town and hamlet made an effort to celebrate the event. Among the St Agnes celebrations was a carnival parade in the evening. The first prize winner in the Decorated Wagon class was the entry 'Flower Girls' by Mrs S.J. Hooper and Miss Mitchell. A photograph held by the writer shows the wagon in the cobbled stable area of Rosemundy House. The connection with the house is not known.

The Adkins were certainly staying at the house in 1912 when, like the Carne family before them, they allowed the Wesleyan tea treat to be held in the grounds. The *West Briton* of the 25th July 1912 recorded: 'Rosemundy grounds were thrown open by Mr and Mrs Adkin who were present to welcome the school'. Also in July Mrs Adkin distributed the prizes at the Regatta and Sports held on the Bank Holiday Monday.

Above: First prize winner in the Decorated Wagon class at the Coronation Carnival 1911.
Below (l-r): Elizabeth Jewell Adkin, Francis Newbery Adkin, Ena Adkin and a family friend.

On the 15ᵗʰ May 1913 the *Royal Cornwall Gazette* reported:

> St Agnes Tennis/Bowling Club opened its season on Friday. Good
> attendance of membership which now stands at 40. The club's existence is
> due to the efforts of Mr & Mrs Adkin of Rosemundy.

In June 1914 the *West Briton* reported:

> St Agnes Band of Hope Festival was held on Whit Monday under
> favourable circumstances ... Through the kindness of Mr and Mrs Adkin
> they were permitted to enter the beautiful grounds of Rosemundy ...

It has been suggested by a now deceased member of the Carne family that
during the First World War the house was used as a convalescent home for
injured servicemen. Although it would have been large enough, with beautiful
gardens in which to recuperate, the writer has been unable to find any record
confirming this suggestion.

In 1919 the house was sold by Mr Adkin to three ladies. The 'Agreemant
Document' held at the Cornwall Record Office (Truro) states:

> Memorandum of Agreement made the twenty third day of September
> One thousand nine hundred and nineteen between Francis Newbery
> Adkin of Westwood, Oaklands Road, Bromley in the County of Kent,
> Esquire of one part, and Lady Mary Trefusis of Porthgwidden in the
> County of Cornwall, Lady Catherine Seward Hain of Treloyhan in the
> County of Cornwall and Francis Jane Bolitho of Trewidden in the county
> of Cornwall, widow, of the other part.

It would appear that like Mr Carne before him, Mr Adkin was very proud
of his garden and plants. His granddaughter told the writer that he loved
gardening and that he gave some of his filmy ferns to Kew Gardens.
She cannot say however whether this happened during his time at
Rosemundy. His love of plants was such that he was not prepared to
leave them all at Rosemundy for the new owners. The following paragraph
appeared in the agreement:

> The vendor reserves the right at any time or times before the first of
> January One thousand nine hundred and twenty one, upon giving
> reasonable notice, to enter upon the premises and remove such of the

ferns and plants (other than fruit trees) which are now growing in the gardens or are planted out in the greenhouses of the said premises as he may select and the purchaser will give an undertaking on completion to the vendor to give facilities for such removal and also not to do or permit any wilful damage to the said ferns and plants so long as any of them remain on the premises as aforesaid.

This clause gave Mr Adkin over twelve months to return and take the plants he wanted from the gardens.

He and his wife went to live in a house at the bottom of Limer's Lane, just outside Bideford, Devon, where again they had a large garden. Elizabeth died there in 1936 and Francis in 1947, aged 86.

Ena Adkin, Francis Newbery Adkin and Elizabeth Jewell Adkin. Note the new front entrance arch.

MOTHER AND BABY HOME

The three ladies were probably not too worried about the garden clause as they had a more important matter to think about, the conversion of the house into the 'Cornwall County Mother and Baby Home'.

Fundraising for the new home started immediately, and in June 1920 an 'American Tea' was held. The *Royal Cornwall Gazette* of the 30th June carried this report:

> An American Tea was held in the grounds of Rosemundy
> on Friday afternoon under the auspices of Lady Mary
> Trefusis, chairman of the Home for mothers and babies. A
> good number responded to the invitation to view the work
> of the committee in caring for the unwanted ones.

In July the following year a 'Pound Day' was held to raise funds. People were invited to visit the home and donate either a pound in money or a pound in weight of something useful, such as food or other groceries.

Babies in cots outside Rosemundy House c. 1922.

General information about the home is contained in the annual reports of the Cornwall Preventive and Rescue Association, which are held at the Cornwall Record Office (X524 Collection). The reports cover the work of the Association from 1921 to 1942, at which point the organisation became the Cornwall Social and Moral Welfare Association.

The first annual report, dated March 31st 1922, starts:

> The Cornwall Preventive and Rescue Association took over the work of the Truro Diocesan Committee twelve months ago, and the past year has been one of great difficulty owing to a variety of different causes, but we hope now that there are signs of increasing interest in the work, and that the future may see a considerable extension of it. In July, 1921 the financial position seemed so desperate that the Council reluctantly recommended the closing of both the Rosemundy and Mount Prospect [Redruth] Homes, but partly owing to the generosity of friends, who raised £127 by a Treasure Sale in September, and partly owing to the generous offer of Miss Roberts to become Lady Superintendent of Rosemundy without any salary and, in addition, to give £200 a year to the work, the Homes were retained. Several changes have been made. The older children at Rosemundy have all been sent to other Homes or to foster parents; the Maternity Home at Mount Prospect has been closed, and girls now go direct to Rosemundy three months before their confinement and remain there nine months afterwards with their babies. The Committee feel that they must adhere to the rule of one year's stay, as no shorter time gives any chance of influencing the girl's [sic] character. The Homes Sub-Committee have parted, with real regret, from Miss Relf, Miss Woodruff, and Nurse Millard, who had all given ungrudging and most valuable work for some years in their different capacities.

There followed a brief report from Miss Relf, covering the period from April 1st 1921 until she left in November:

> 5 girls and their babies were admitted from Mount Prospect, and 8 girls left, having remained for periods varying from 3 to 18 months. The average number of mothers with their babies was 8, and, in addition, there were 17 older children.

Rosemundy House staff in the early 1920s.

Miss Roberts then reported on the period from November 1921 to March 31st 1922:

> ... the probationers left before Christmas, and ... in January there was a new staff consisting of Assistant Matron, Laundry Matron, Kitchen Matron, and two nurses. The older children have all been sent to homes or foster parents. There are now 10 mothers and 9 babies in the Home, and the first confinement took place in February.

Children's play area in the gardens in the early 1920s.

APRIL 1ST 1922 TO MARCH 31ST 1923

Miss Roberts remained Lady Superintendent for this year and in March 1923 gave her annual report to the Cornwall Preventive and Rescue Association:

> 27 girls have been helped by this Home in the past year: 18 have been admitted since March, 1922 ... At the present time we have 17 girls and 13 babies in the Home. We have found situations for eleven, who on the whole are doing well ... In each case the girl pays for the maintenance of her child with a foster mother (part payment where an affiliation order has been obtained) and she is able to visit it in her spare time. The separation is felt very keenly, as without exception, the mothers really care for their children. Everything is done that is possible to foster this love and to make them realise their responsibility for the child. A special point is made of trying to find a situation for the mother near her child, or a home for the child near its mother ... The health of the household has been good. Several small and delicate babies have picked up wonderfully and promise to become strong children.

APRIL 1ST 1923 TO MARCH 31ST 1924

Miss Roberts again submitted her report:

> We have had a very full and busy year: 34 girls have been through the Home, of whom 12 have been placed in situations, 3 left to go home, one left to be married; 17 new girls have been admitted ... At present there are 17 girls and 10 babies ... The difficulty of finding good foster mothers increases, and to find them within reasonable distance of the mother's work is sometimes almost impossible ... There has been marked improvement in the work and character of the majority of girls in the home: a great deal of the value of the work done is due to the loyalty and energy of the staff ... The girls who have left are doing well on the whole, and those within easy distance come and visit us from time to time. Two came for a short holiday last summer, one from Devonshire and one from London, and they were grateful for what the Home had done for them ...

The annual report ended: 'For admittance to the home, apply to the Lady Superintendent: the charges are 10/- to 12/- [50p to 60p] weekly for Cornish girls, 15/- [75p] for those outside of Cornwall'. (These charges remained the same for several years.)

In August 1923 a fete was held, but it was apparently not very successful. The *Royal Cornwall Gazette* carried this report:

> With so many claims made during the past few weeks, the appeal on behalf of the Children's Home was not so successful as usual. The amount secured was £3.

APRIL 1ST 1924 TO MARCH 31ST 1925

Miss Roberts' report:

> The Home has been full all the year; at the moment of writing there are 18 girls and 14 babies. For April, 1924, we had 17 girls in the Home; 19 were admitted during the following months, making 36 in all who have received help. If the girls stay a full year, a good situation is found for them, and if necessary, an outfit, made in the Home, is provided for

them ... Situations were found for 13 girls, and they are ... doing well ... Five went to live at home with their babies ... The most important change has been made in the garden. We now have a lady gardener, and the girls who are able to do so, work under her, which is beneficial both to health and character ... Affiliation orders are always difficult to obtain through lack of corroborative evidence; but payment has been secured for eight mothers from the fathers of the children.

In 1925 Miss Roberts retired to a cottage in Guernsey. In 1958 she was interviewed at her home. This interview appears in the *Gwendroc Paper, Number 11. Moral Welfare Work in Cornwall,* held in the Courtney Library at the Royal Institution of Cornwall, Truro. She tells of her time at Rosemundy:

The rule in Rosemundy Home at that time was that girls should come in three months before confinement and remain there for the ensuing nine months with their babies. It was felt that at least twelve months must be spent in forming character. The girls were also trained in baby care, cooking, housekeeping and sewing. So far as sewing was concerned they were taught plain dressmaking and then Miss Margaret Smith, who was a renowned 'fancy-work' needlewoman, taught them honeycombing and smocking. The babies at Rosemundy went outdoors 'as if they came out of a band box' as the righteous-overmuch were prone to protest ... The employed staff consisted of an assistant matron, a laundry matron, a kitchen matron and two nurses. This strange un-Cornish use of titles was a compensation for sadly inadequate salaries, it was openly said. The nurses were better paid, as they had been better trained. There was a certain amount of internecine strife. What was to be expected where employment itself was uncertain from month to month and where pay and conditions were all but humiliating? Among the indoor and outdoor staff frail pettiness was found alongside the nobility of personal sacrifice.

Rock garden in the early 1920s. Written on the rear of the postcard is 'where we walk the babies up and down'.

APRIL 1ST 1925 TO MARCH 31ST 1926

Miss Florence Hughes, who replaced Miss Roberts as Lady Superintendent, reported:

> The Home has been well used during the year; sixteen girls were in the home at the beginning of April 1925; eighteen were admitted during the following twelve months, making a total of 34. A good situation is found for all girls who remain their full year, and where necessary, an outfit, made at Rosemundy, is given ... Last year, situations were found for 11 girls, most of whom are doing well: 4 girls went to live at home with their babies, and one we are sorry to report, died in hospital. One baby (premature) died in the home. The general health at Rosemundy has been good.

APRIL 1ˢᵀ 1926 TO MARCH 31ˢᵀ 1927

This year Miss Hughes was replaced by Miss Ruth Oates as Lady Superintendent. She reported:

> In April, 1926, there were 15 girls at the Home; nine were admitted during the following months, making a total of twenty-five [sic]. At the time of writing there are 14 girls and 10 babies in the Home ... While in the Home the girls are taught plain cooking, washing and ironing and the making of simple garments. Those who are able do some work in the garden under the direction of the lady gardener. The general health of all during the year has been good.

APRIL 1ˢᵀ 1927 TO MARCH 31ˢᵀ 1928

Miss Oates submitted her report for the year:

> The year has been a busy one. At the time of writing there are 17 girls and 14 babies in the Home. For April of last year there were 12 girls, 8 of whom were placed in situations and are doing well. 4 left to go home. Altogether during the year 29 girls have received help. The girls stay for one year and on leaving are placed in situations, and [sic] outfit provided when necessary, and a foster-mother found for the baby. Finding suitable foster-mothers is a difficulty as it is essential that the child should be placed within a reasonable distance of the mother's work. Affiliation Orders are taken out whenever sufficient legal evidence can be produced. Dr. Barnardo's grant has been obtained for two mothers. The girls often remark how quickly the days pass – it is perhaps because the days are reasonably full without being unduly busy. Each mother, under the direction of a trained nurse, looks after her own baby. She has also a portion of work to do in the Home. The afternoons (weather permitting) are spent in the garden, when those who are able do a little gardening under the direction of a lady gardener, and two hours of five evenings in the week are given to sewing – when the girls help with their own outfit and that of their baby. Regular religious instruction is also given. The health of all on the whole has been quite good, and now there is the new

shelter in the garden we hope that in future the health of the babies will be such as to leave nothing to be desired. We are very grateful to those who have sent gifts of clothing, etc., and we are always glad of old linen and shoes.

APRIL 1ST 1928 TO MARCH 31ST 1929

Miss Margaret Mitchell, Lady Superintendent, submitted her report for the year:

Twenty-eight girls have passed through the Home during the past year. Twenty-six babies have been born in the Home, every one of them now bonny healthy babies. Seven of the girls who have left during the year have been able to take their babies home with them. The other girls have had situations found for them and foster mothers for their babies. We are so very grateful when we can find a mistress who will take mother and baby; the mistress generally benefits, the mother gives her very best because she is so grateful, and our babies really are well trained. We try very hard during the year the girls are with us to strengthen them spiritually, morally and physically; to teach them to look at life from quite a different standpoint and to value themselves and their future. We believe that much is gained in the moral and physical training of our girls by the fact that each mother does everything for her own baby; all our babies are breast fed; each mother takes care of her own baby at night, she learns how to wash, sew and knit for her baby, and this, with the learning of good housewifery and close contact with our beautiful garden helps to make real women of our girls. We gratefully thank friends who have sent us gifts of clothing, house linen, baby woollies, etc. As we have let our vegetable garden we shall be very grateful for any gifts of fruit or vegetables.

A group of babies in 1929.

APRIL 1ST 1929 TO MARCH 31ST 1930

Miss Mitchell again submitted her report:

> Fifteen fresh cases have been admitted during the year, making with six
> already in the Home twenty-one girls altogether for the year. Thirteen
> babies have been born during the year. Five babies have gone home
> with their mothers at the end of their mothers' year, one has gone with
> the mother into service and five have been fostered. The past year has
> not been an easy one, there has been so much sickness amongst both
> mothers and babies due entirely to pre-natal conditions. One feels very
> grateful for the perfect conditions at Rosemundy, which help us so much
> to discharge mothers and babies in an excellent state of health. Our girls
> come to us often so destitute of any idea of the meaning of real home
> life – so unaware of how interesting housework, gardening and sewing
> can become. Nearly all of them gradually realise that the days just spent
> in doing their work well give much happiness. We have had in the home
> this year one or two intensely sad cases. We wish so much that there were
> in the world more wisely loving mothers; so many of our saddest cases
> are due to the lack of understanding and home training. Our girls are
> so willing to be taught the management of their babies that they become

very wise and controlled little mothers; we wish we had them longer with us. We are very grateful to all the friends who, this year, have so kindly sent us gifts. May we beg for wool for baby garments; also for fruit and vegetables.

APRIL 1ST 1930 TO MARCH 31ST 1931

Margaret Mitchell's report for the year:

Sixteen girls have been received during the past year, making with eight already in the Home twenty-four altogether. Seventeen babies have been born during the year. Of these nine were very much under the average weight at birth and needed exceptional care. One died. The others are now perfectly healthy, normal babies. Four of the girls leaving in the past year have been able to take their babies with them; the others have been fostered in as good homes as we could find for them.

The past year has been a very happy one at Rosemundy. The girls seem really to appreciate the Home and all it stands for: and on the whole they do try to learn the work of the Home in its various departments. It is surprising to see what discipline, happiness and a healthy environment can do for them. Three who were admitted this year were said to be mentally weak, but in each case they have so much improved that they are now healthy, happy girls and good mothers, very much in love with their babies.

We are very happy in the visits of our old girls to Rosemundy. So many of them come back to us on their half days. It is amazing how much they will sacrifice for their babies. When they badly need new clothes for themselves their babies come first. They rarely spend money on pictures or such luxuries.

We feel that our work is tested when they go out into situations and we consider we have failed with them if they do not keep their places, or are unsatisfactory. I am glad to be able to say that complaints are rare.

There are people who suggest that money and strength are thrown away in this work – but those of us who are in it know that they are mistaken and that the more you know of it the more you want to help it because of those whose lives are made anew, who face the future in a way they had never learned to face life before.

We are grateful for gifts from Sewing Guilds, and from personal friends of the Home – especially for three beautiful cots from Mr. and Mrs. James Christie.

APRIL 1ST 1931 TO MARCH 31ST 1932

Report for the year:

There were fourteen girls in the Home when the year began and there have been twenty-one admissions during the year. Of these, five required special treatment, so that their babies were born at Exeter, but they returned to us for training. Exactly half the girls in the Home this year have been under eighteen and four of them were mere children to whom everything had to be explained. They had had no moral training and their minds were open to any kind of influence. Unfortunately, bad influences came all too soon, and we did not get to know the girls until disaster had resulted. These younger girls generally settle down very happily with us and we find that quite often their mothers are anxious to help us to repair the damage done by lack of moral education.

Much the same is true of the older girls. They have been led astray because they had only learnt about sex from wrong sources and never grasped the need for self-control. The improvement in their behaviour and conversation after they have been with us some time, is so marked that we realise how finely they might have developed if they had always been under good influences.

Nearly all our old girls are doing well and are a source of joy to us. On their behalf we should like to acknowledge with gratitude the services of our Honorary Solicitor, Mr. Donald Thomas. We should also like to pay our tribute to the great value of the assistance that some of them receive from Dr. Barnardo's Auxiliary Fund, which, in certain approved cases, where the whole sum could not otherwise be raised, helps the young mother to pay the foster mother's weekly charge for the maintenance of the baby. We should also like to mention with gratitude the help given by some doctors in attending these boarded out babies free of charge.

Visitors to Rosemundy often remark on the happy appearance of the girls; we are quite sure that this is not because they have forgotten the reason for their being there, but because for the first time in the lives of many they breathe an atmosphere of real love and unselfishness under discipline. Even before realising the source of that atmosphere in the Home, they enter into its spirit and are content.

After the first two or three months of her stay we rarely hear a girl express a wish that her time at Rosemundy were up, and by the end of their year nearly all are loth to go.

The Secrets of Rosemundy House

It is quite remarkable to see how readily new arrivals adapt themselves to the routine of the house. Each has three month's training in the four departments, nursery, laundry, kitchen and house-parlour work. They are proud to do well so that they may be promoted to the next department. Under this system we are able to find out a girl's special qualities and when she goes to a situation, we seek to place her accordingly.

Nothing in the training of the girls seems to us more important than that, what is done for their religious life in the Home, shall be lasting, and we do our best to make the daily service in the Home and the Bible Class so suit their needs that their influence will endure. The girls also have weekly classes with the Chaplains and we cannot be too grateful to them for their continued and regular help with this side of the work. They also write to the clergyman or minister of the place to which each girl is going when she leaves the Home. But even so many of our girls find it difficult to attend a strange Church, and it would be a great help if Church members would show some friendship to the new-comer, without, of course, making her a marked person.

We tender grateful thanks to the Needlework Guilds, to members of the committee and other friends for gifts of clothing, blankets, household linen, a bedstead and mattress, hardware and babies' woollies and other useful gifts received during the year.

APRIL 1ST 1932 TO MARCH 31ST 1933

Report for the year:

Eight girls were in the Home at the beginning of the year and there have been 19 admitted during the year, making a total of 27 who have been in the Home for some part of the year under review.

Two girls requiring treatment were sent to Exeter, where their babies were born. In another case, where [an] operation was necessary, the girl was admitted to Redruth Hospital, returning later to the Home for training, bringing her baby with her.

During the greater part of the year the health of the Home was good, but in the end of January we did not escape the influenza epidemic, and we are sorry to report that during it one of our delicate babies died.

Seven girls, at the conclusion of their training, have been able to place their babies in the charge of their parents. For the others, trustworthy foster parents have been found. The girls themselves, except where health made it impossible, have gone into service, and practically all are doing well, and are good mothers to their babies, proving the use of the period they spent together in the Home.

We are grateful to the Honorary Chaplains, the Rev. W.T. Andrews and the Rev. F. G. Gray, for their weekly classes and the kindly interest taken in each individual girl.

We are also much indebted to our Honorary Solicitor, Mr. Donald Thomas, who in seven cases has been successful in getting payments towards babies' maintenance from their fathers. Three cases were dealt with by private agreement, and in four others affiliation orders were obtained in court.

Gifts from kind friends have been much appreciated. We are particularly grateful to Miss Hosgood for materials for making babies' outfits, given at regular intervals, and also to Miss Agnew for a regular gift of vegetables, and to Miss Roberts for her continual kindness in using her car for the Home when there are girls to be fetched or to go for treatment.

APRIL 1ST 1933 TO MARCH 31ST 1934

Miss D. Neve, Matron, submitted her report for the year:

30 girls have passed through the Home during the twelve months. 13 babies have been born and 6 mothers have been admitted with their babies. 3 girls have been able to take their babies home with them. Situations have been found for other mothers, and foster homes for their babies. 1 mother with her child has gone to live with relations in Australia. In 4 cases we have been able to make the fathers pay towards the maintenance of their babies. In these, and in other cases, our thanks are due to our Honorary Solicitor.

We are also grateful to Dr Barnardo's Homes for the generous assistance towards the maintenance of those babies whose mothers are unable to obtain other help.

During September a fête was held in Rosemundy garden, and we are extremely grateful to those friends who helped to make it a success. It was pleasant to find that those of the former Rosemundy Home girls who were in a position to do so, showed their appreciation of the home by bringing articles for the stalls and also helping with the teas.

The *Royal Cornwall Gazette* of the 13th September recorded the event. Under the heading 'Cornwall Social Welfare Work' its report read:

> In aid of the funds of Cornwall Preventive and Rescue Association a very successful fete was held in the grounds of Rosemundy, St Agnes, on Friday afternoon.
>
> Beautiful weather favoured this annual event and there was a large attendance. There were a large number of stalls of every description and sideshows, and in the evening the play "When the Queen passed by" was given by members of the St Agnes Women's Institute. The fete was opened by Lady Jean Petherick who was introduced by Miss Margaret Smith. Mrs Charles Treffry proposed a vote of thanks to Lady Jean Petherick and remarked that it was the late Mary Trefusis who persuaded her to take up the work and during the last nine years they had cleared a tremendous amount of money. Major G. Gilpin seconded the vote of thanks.
>
> Those taking part in the play "When the Queen passed by," were Mesdames A. Harris, Moore, Winsor and Ferris, the misses M.A. Bartle, Pollett, Parnell, V. Whitta, V. and B. Harris, M. Parnell, D. Keast, Wilson, J. Barkle and masters J. Higgins, K. Winsor and F. Keast. Mrs Baker was the pianist.

The annual report continued:

> Towards the end of [1933], an outbreak of whooping cough amongst the babies was the cause of a great deal of anxiety, and of an unavoidable increase in expenditure. Six of the babies were ill, but all made good recovery and are now bonny children.
>
> The general routine of the Home allows each girl to receive training in laundry, cooking, house parlour work and mothercraft. When leaving the Home a situation is found for her in accordance with her capability.
>
> Each girl does everything for her baby. This encourages all that is best in them and makes them more conscious of the need of religion in everyday life and more open to good influences round them. Daily services and the girls' Bible Classes are carefully planned in the hope that the realisation of the presence of God may become stronger throughout their lives. The girls' appreciation of the weekly Bible Classes is the best thanks that can be given to the Chaplains for their regular visits. Three girls have been confirmed during the year.
>
> We are grateful to those friends who have so kindly sent gifts to the Home, and to all those who in other ways have shown their interest.

APRIL 1ST 1934 TO MARCH 31ST 1935

Miss D. Neve submitted her report for the year:

> 37 girls and 33 babies have passed through the Home. Of the former, four were under the age of 17 years, and twenty-three between that age and 21 years. These young mothers, usually untrained and quite uncontrolled, find it difficult to submit to the prospect of twelve months of ordered life; yet in most cases they settle down quite happily. Then with the birth of the baby comes the dawning realisation that life is not solely an opportunity for self-gratification; and the development of such consciousness is aided considerably by the daily routine of serving a helpless baby.
>
> Training in all departments of housekeeping must be given that each girl may become capable of earning sufficient wages to maintain both herself and her baby. Nursery, laundry, kitchen and house-parlour work are taken in turn so that, later, a situation may be found for each girl in accordance with her special qualities.
>
> The making of baby clothes, epecially the outfits for use when leaving, which each girl, so far as is possible, makes for her own baby, arouses an interest in needlework.
>
> Much could be said of the steady growth in a consciousness of spiritual and moral values which in so many cases, marks the last months of a girl's time in the Home.
>
> The daily services and the weekly Bible classes all aim at giving strength to face the world when the twelve months are ended.
>
> It may here be mentioned that five girls were confirmed during the last twelve months.
>
> Practically all the old girls are doing well. Three have married since leaving the Home and taken their babies to their new homes.
>
> Two others were married after their babies were born in Rosemundy. Those who were able to do so gave small articles to be sold at the summer fete, also gifts to the Home at Christmas.
>
> After the expenses of a foster mother and the child's clothing have been covered it is only in a very few cases that there is even a small margin for any material expression of appreciation.

In this connection we are glad to express our gratitude to the Managers of Dr Barna[r]do's Auxiliary Fund for the help so kindly given to recommended cases in which it is impossible for the entire weekly charge of the foster mother to be paid by the mother.

We give grateful thanks to the Needlework Guilds and friends who have made gifts of clothing, baby woollies, etc.

As in so many cases the girls' relatives are too poor to provide clothes for so long a period as twelve months we are in real need of further gifts of shoes, stockings and other articles of clothing.

APRIL 1ST 1935 TO MARCH 31ST 1936

Miss D. Neve again submitted her report:

During the past year we have again had evidence of the number of very young girls who need the shelter of such a Home as Rosemundy. Of the 23 girls who have stayed in the Home 4 are under 17 years of age, and 8 between 17 and 20 years old. The youngest of these mothers present a very special and difficult problem. They love their children with an affection equal to that which any older and more happily situated mother may feel. But some of them are not sufficiently matured to earn their living with the additional responsibility of a child. We have had to allow one or two of these younger mothers to remain for longer than the usual period in the Home. It is hoped later to find them situations with employers who will take a protective interest in their welfare. Four of the girls who have finished their training in Rosemundy have been able to take their babies home, and have themselves gone out to work.

After-care is by no means the least important activity of the Home. It is not easy for any girl to support herself and her child. She needs encouragement of a kind which can only be given by someone who, knowing all the circumstances, can understand the individual difficulties which each girl inevitably meets.

Perhaps the greatest proof of the usefulness of Rosemundy is given by those girls who, having accepted the help offered by the Home, have there learned their children's need of them and willingly give all they can that the children may be happy.

Suitable foster mothers are not easy to find, but we have several happy homes where the foster mothers are willing to co-operate with the matron by welcoming the mother in her free time, and allowing her to feel that the child's home is also her own home.

On the 19th July 1935 the St Agnes School Log Book recorded that the whole school was given the afternoon off to attend the fete at Rosemundy.

APRIL 1ST 1936 TO MARCH 31ST 1937

Miss E.M. McLeod took over as Matron on May 29th 1936. The annual report of Miss Margaret E. Smith, Chairman of the Home Sub-Committee, included the following:

> Rosemundy has been full throughout the year. At the end of March there were 17 girls and 5 babies in the Home and 16 girls have passed out of the Home during the year. 8 of these went to situations found for them from the Home, 3 went home, 4 who were very young were passed on to other Homes, and 1 who was mentally unstable was passed to the care of the Public Assistance Committee.
>
> Sixteen babies were born in the Home. One was still-born and one only lived a fortnight. Five other babies were born at Exeter, where we had been obliged to send the mothers for special treatment; these mothers and babies return to us as soon as they can safely do so. The love and care which is bestowed on the babies by Sister and other members of the staff is rewarded by the wonderful progress which they make. Many a puny infant over whom we have shaken our heads has developed into a bonny little person by the time he is nine months old and ready to leave the Home.
>
> When the mothers go into service these babies go to foster mothers and we are always glad of those who will help us to find kind and reliable foster mothers.
>
> The Home is much indebted to the Anglican and Nonconformist chaplains, the Rev. W.T. Andrews and Rev. A. Trevellick Cape, who visit weekly and hold classes with the girls. Four girls have been confirmed this year.

Miss McLeod has also been grateful to others who have taken an interest in the girls, especially to Miss Oates who comes in to take Folk Dancing with them and to those who have helped her with transport.

She would like to express her thanks, too, for many gifts, including a piano, an extra bath, books, bedding, garments, shoes, curtains, and vegetables, and for a money gift towards much needed linoleum for the nursery floor, which we cannot afford at present. She would also be grateful for suitable story books and for strong shoes.

Mothers in the summer of 1936.

APRIL 1ST 1937 TO MARCH 31ST 1938

Annual report:

> Miss McLeod reports that 30 girls have been in the Home during the
> past year and that 4 old girls came for holidays. Three girls were passed
> on to other institutions for reasons of health. Of those who left 15 went
> to service, 3 went home and 1 went to a Hostel where she could work and
> have her baby with her.
>
> Five affiliation cases have been taken into court, four of which have
> been won and one lost. Two private agreements have also been made.
> The health of the Home has been excellent throughout the year. The
> girls were most grateful to Miss Oates and Miss Vanstone for the Folk
> Dancing Classes, to Miss Howson for the First Aid Classes, and to Miss
> James for coming in to play to them.
>
> Two girls have been confirmed this year.
>
> Miss McLeod would like to express her gratitude to the Cornwall
> Needlework Guild for useful parcels, to the Churches which sent fruit
> and vegetables from their Harvest Thanksgivings, to Mrs. Thynne for a
> welcome gift of mats, to the Hon. Secretary [Mrs Ashley Rowe] for baby
> clothes, to Miss Roberts for so frequently using her car for the Home,
> and to many others for gifts of newspapers, clothing and Christmas gifts
> which have been much appreciated.
>
> There is no gift more needed than that of shoes for the girls. A hearthrug
> for the dining-room would also be appreciated.

In 1937, under the heading 'Cornwall Preventive Association', the *Royal
Cornwall Gazette* of the 28th July reported:

> The sum of £46 was raised in aid of the Rosemundy Home, St Agnes
> on Friday by a garden fete organised in the grounds of the Home by
> the Cornwall Preventive Association. Presiding at the opening Miss
> Margaret Smith (Chairman of the Home sub-committee) explained the
> work of the home.
>
> Miss Skilbeck (Bodmin) who opened the fete said the home did
> great work for mothers and restored them to their rightful place as
> homemakers. She was thanked by Mrs Ashley Rowe (Hon. Secretary of
> the Home sub-committee).

The most popular feature of the fete was a thriller play, "Mystery Cottage" presented by Perranporth Players. A folk dance display was given by St Agnes Ladies Hockey Club under Miss Oats, music being supplied by Mrs Baker. St Agnes orchestra under Mr F. Brogden played a selection during the afternoon.

APRIL 1ST 1938 TO MARCH 31ST 1939

Annual report:

Miss McLeod reports that 27 girls and 24 babies have been in the Home during the year and 4 old girls came for holidays. The Home was not very full last summer – but at present there are 16 girls and 15 babies, which is almost a record number.

Five affiliation cases have been taken into Court, four of which were won, and one lost. In addition to this, three private agreements have been arranged.

Miss McLeod keeps in touch with her old girls, as much as possible. Four of them have been married during the year. The great majority prove themselves able to take their place in the world satisfactorily when they have had a year's training in the Home. The only girls who have lapsed recently have been those whom we were unable to get certified as mentally deficient when they were in the Home, but whose mental conditions gave us cause for anxiety.

Our gratitude is due to both the chaplains for their continued help, to those who have given us legal help, to Dr [Cuthbert] Whitworth for the classes in first aid which he has given, to Miss Oates and Miss Vanstone who have taken Folk Dancing Classes, and Miss James who has played to the girls, to the Churches who have sent gifts from the Harvest Thanksgivings, to the Cornwall Needlework Guild, the Caerhays Working Party, St. Agnes Wesley Guild for presents of garments, to the Honorary Secretary for baby clothes, to an anonymous donor for Christmas presents, and to Mrs. Money for arranging a picnic.

APRIL 1ST 1939 TO MARCH 31ST 1940

Annual report:

The Home at Rosemundy continues its work for unmarried mothers and their babies. Including 10 girls who were in the Home at the end of the year, there have been 33 girls in the Home in the course of the year, and 26 babies. Two girls came back to spend their holidays in the Home. Eleven have gone out to service during the year, 1 was married, seven were passed on to other institutions, and four went home.

Some of the girls admitted are very young and irresponsible and their training and after care bring special problems.

The Home Committee wish to express their gratitude for useful articles from the Cornwall Needlework Guild, and to kind friends who send baby clothes, garden produce and papers, and to those who remembered the Home at Christmas.

Of all gifts, shoes for the girls are amongst the most acceptable.

Our thanks are due to Dr. Whitworth for his many kindnesses to the Home, and to Mr. Gibson and Mr. Pelloe for their legal advice.

APRIL 1ST 1940 TO MARCH 31ST 1941

Annual report of the Secretary, Mrs Ford:

Owing to war conditions we are not printing the whole of the report which was read at the Annual Meeting. Yet we feel that subscribers should be informed that at one point in the year 1940-41 our overdraft was such that the Committee considered closing the Home at Rosemundy. The need for Maternity beds, however, was so great that the County Council has come to our rescue with a temporarily increased grant for which the Committee is most grateful. This does not, however, alter the fact that to carry on our work we need to increase our income by £200 a year. If the Parish Contributions, which last year dwindled to £24, could bring in again the £143 which they did in 1934, and if every member of our committee would find a new subscriber we should be well on our way to achieving this object.

Our Children's Welfare Workers, Miss Kent and Miss Matthews, both report increased pressure of work owing to war conditions. Miss Kent has dealt with 69 new and 165 old cases. Miss Matthews, in the six months since she took over Miss Bence's work has dealt with 33 new and 120 old cases. Miss Bence had dealt with 41 new cases in the previous six months.

In Rosemundy there have been 33 girls, and there are increased applications from Cornwall, as well as those from areas where the Maternity Homes have been evacuated.

The war has brought greater need for every branch of our work. Please help us to meet the need.

APRIL 1ST 1941 TO MARCH 31ST 1942

The annual report is missing from the records. During this period the name of the organisation that ran the Home changed from the Cornwall Preventive and Rescue Association to the Cornwall Social and Moral Welfare Association.

APRIL 1ST 1942 TO MARCH 31ST 1943

Annual report:

> There have been 32 babies and 46 girls in the Home during the year, beside 4 old girls who came for holidays.
>
> This is a larger number than usual, for under War conditions girls do not stay so long in the Home. 8 left for War work, 8 went into domestic service with their babies, 6 went to friends, 8 to Hospital, 1 to the Public Assistance Institution, 2 to Home, 2 were married, 1 refused help, and 10 were still in the Home at the end of the year.
>
> War conditions not only increase the number of girls needing our help, but they add to the problem of dealing with them, for it is difficult for them to settle down to nursing their babies and doing housework, when all their friends are finding more exciting activities.
>
> Miss McLeod wishes to thank all those who have sent gifts. She is most grateful for the help given by the Needlework Guild, and the W.V.S. in supplying layettes.

APRIL 1ST 1943 TO MARCH 31ST 1944

Annual report:

> 58 girls have been in the Home during the year. Miss McLeod felt it to be an exceptionally difficult time. There was a restless atmosphere, in which it was hard to do constructive work. Many of the girls coming into the Home had been leading rather exciting lives in conditions that were new to them. They missed these excitements in the Home, and wished to stay as short a time as possible. The ample opportunities for even the least efficient to earn good wages made it seem to them silly to stay in the Home and learn to look after their babies, and unfortunately their mothers agreed.

> The Committee found that a short time of stay did not give the Home time to give the girls a changed attitude, or the babies a fair start in life – and they made it a rule that no girl must be admitted who was not prepared to stay for at least six months after the birth of her child. The girls who are in the Home at present have all come in on that understanding, and the Home is quite full.

> Miss McLeod, to whose unselfishness and devotion we should like to pay tribute, left us recently after being eight years in charge of the Home. We welcome in her place Miss Ackroyd, and wish her and her staff happiness and real success in the work of the Home. We should like to thank the Chaplains and all those who have helped the Home by their gifts and their interest.

APRIL 1ST 1944 TO MARCH 31ST 1945

Miss Barbara Ackroyd submitted her annual report:

> The past twelve months have brought many changes to Rosemundy, changes of person[n]el, of policy and of administration. One can hardly assess the results of these changes in so short a time, but I think it is true to say that the 41 girls who, with their babies, have stayed in the Home for a period of not less than 7 months, have all been happy and contented; have learnt a great deal of housecraft and baby welfare, and have benefited by their stay, physically, morally and spiritually.

Nine of the girls have gone to situations with their babies, and are settled and doing well. Fourteen of them have gone to their own homes, either taking their babies with them, or in one or two cases placing them with foster-mothers. Two girls have been married, and one has returned to us as a member of staff bringing her baby with her. The remaining 15 were still in the Home at the end of the year.

We have had classes taken throughout the year by the Vicar of the parish, who is also Chaplain to the Home, and by the Nonconformist Minister, to both of whom we owe a great debt of gratitude. Six of the girls have been confirmed at their own request.

We would like to express our gratitude to the many friends who have helped us, and above all to the Committee whose unfailing sympathy and support has helped us through what has been a very difficult year, but one full of interest, and of progress in the lives of so many.

APRIL 1ST 1945 TO MARCH 31ST 1946

Miss Ackroyd again submitted her annual report:

This year has produced many difficulties, owing to shortage of staff, and for the greater part of the year, we have been without kitchen or laundry matrons.

But the Home has always been full, and 31 girls and 23 babies have been helped during the year. The pressure on our beds was so great, that a new wing has been opened, and we can now take 22 girls. We hope to take another four in the near future.

We shall be very grateful for gifts towards the fitting up of these new rooms. It may help our friends to know that if they like to give us towels, etc., we can supply the necessary coupons.

It is interesting to see how the majority of girls come to the Home with fixed ideas about the necessity of adoption for their children, and how nearly all of them find that mother love is stronger than their fixed ideas and that therefore, adoption, or even separation from their babies is impossible.

The courageous way in which they tackle their responsibilities deserves our wholehearted admiration, and help, and above all, our prayers.

We owe a very sincere debt of gratitude to all those people who have helped us so generously in many ways. It would be impossible to enumerate them, but we would especially like to thank our Chaplains, and medical attendants, and not least, the Home Committee, who are unfailing in their help and interest.

APRIL 1ST 1946 TO MARCH 31ST 1947

The annual report showed that 39 girls and 39 babies were admitted. As to the destinations of the girls, 20 went home or to friends, six to situations, two to other homes and eleven were still in the Home on March 31st. Of the babies, 16 were with their mothers, five were adopted, three went to foster parents, three to other Homes and one died. Eleven remained in the Home. The report continued:

> Statistics are often uninteresting, and do not always shew [show] clearly the true state of affairs, but they are sometimes helpful in considering reports. In 1944 and 1945 the average age of the girls was 19, 31, and 19, 23 years respectively, but in 1946 the average age has risen to 21, 31 years. The figures also shew two points which give food for thought. Out of 39 girls admitted during the year, 11 were over the age of 25, and seven were under 17. Does this not shew the great need for more education? One would not suggest that education would prevent undisciplined behaviour, but I feel sure that if more sex education were given in schools and clubs, and places where young people congregate, much could be done to allay the curiosity which is usually the cause of the position in which these young girls have found themselves.
>
> The number of girls of over 25 causes a good deal of sadness, because it is usually a case of genuine affection for the father of the child who, in so many cases, only admits he is married when the girl finds herself to be pregnant.

APRIL 1ST 1947 TO MARCH 31ST 1948

Miss Ackroyd submitted her report:

During the year we have dealt with 40 girls and 35 babies, of these babies 6 went to adopting parents, and with the exception of three, who were placed with foster parents, all the others went with their mothers either home, or to situations.

This does not sound a very formidable list, but it represents an amazing variety of problems, which have to be sorted out, and dealt with. Many people imagine that, with the new regulations for the well being of mothers and babies, any mother can get all the help she needs, through the official channels, but all of these girls in our homes, are those who, for one reason or another, fall outside the scope of the statutory social services, and need specialised help.

It is in giving this specialised help that our most important work lies. It is not sufficient to see that the physical needs are met and dealt with, important though they are – that part of the work is comparatively easy. But it is essential that everything possible should be done to meet the mental and spiritual needs. When these have been met, however inadequately, something has been done towards the re-establishment of a girl in society, which is one of our chief aims.

This task is made more difficult by the shortage of staff, and that is still one of our great problems, but I would like to express my gratitude to the staff we have got, for their unswerving loyalty and help.

At the same time, our grateful thanks are due to those whom we are pleased to call our friends, amongst them the Chaplain, the Rev. G.H. Barnicoat and Dr. Robb, The St. Agnes Parochial Church Council, and the St. Agnes Women's Institute, and countless other people, too numerous to be mentioned by name, both of St. Agnes and a wider field, who have done so much to help us during the past year.

APRIL 1ST 1948 TO MARCH 31ST 1949

Fifty-two girls and 44 babies were dealt with; 36 girls went to their own homes or to friends, 12 went to situations and 4 to other homes; 30 babies went with their mothers, 8 to adopting parents, 4 to nurseries and 2 to foster parents. Miss Ackroyd's report continued:

> The year 1948-49 has been a momentous year for Rosemundy in more than one way. The foregoing figures may be allowed to speak for themselves; whilst a short description is given of the changes which have taken place in the Home.
>
> The outside of the house has been painted, and now has a welcoming appearance for all who come, inside improvements, long needed, have been made, walls have been cleaned and distempered, and some new furniture has been bought for the girls' room. These improvements

Mothers in 1948.

which make such a difference to the general atmosphere, have been made possible by the work, and generosity of our many friends and neighbours who have worked for us, and have shown their interest in so many ways, as well as by the help of the Committee.

The B.B.C. broadcast on January 2nd, 1949, has widened our circle of friends, and we shall always be grateful for the means which made it possible to achieve such ends.

The girls who come to us, often with fears and anxieties created by their particular problem, are not less than in former years, but more, and this is a problem in itself for all who are concerned with modern society. At Rosemundy, we try not only to allay their fears, but also to re-direct their attitude towards themselves, and others.

This part of our work cannot be put into words, but it is the more exacting part, and demands from the staff, and all those who live at Rosemundy, great discernment and courage.

We have been fortunate during the past year, in having a staff who have given of their best, and I would like to pay tribute to them, and to all those who have made 1948-49 so happy a year.

APRIL 1ˢᵀ 1949 TO MARCH 31ˢᵀ 1950

Statistics for the year: 63 girls and 52 babies dealt with; 28 girls went to their own homes or to friends, 14 to situations, 2 to other homes and 19 were still at the Home; 33 babies were kept with their mothers, 10 went to adopting parents, 8 to nurseries and 1 to a foster mother. Miss Ackroyd reported:

1949-1950 has been a year of much activity, hard work, and of the usual ups and downs, but taking all in all, a year of definite growth. Partly perhaps because of the closing of so many voluntary Homes in other counties, we have been asked to take more girls than usual from out of Cornwall, and for the first time for several years the house was full to capacity for the whole twelve months. Preference is always given, however, to Cornish girls, and the need for the Home appears to be as great, if not greater than ever.

In these days, when self discipline and self restraint are not considered important, it can be a matter for real happiness, that so many of our girls have the courage to accept their responsibilities and in spite of all the hardships involved in this course, have made, or are making, good homes for themselves and their children.

Sometimes people fail to recognise how much care and help the girls still need, after they have left the home, and it made one both sad and happy to hear a group of old girls say, when they met together at Christmastide, that they wished they could come back to Rosemundy.

Over the years, Rosemundy has had good times and bad, but it still stands for something solid and permanent in the lives of many who have gone away and who are struggling to make happy lives for their children.

Through the generosity of many friends both old and new, we have been able to make several additions and improvements to the Home and for the first time for years, the garden really begins to look cared for.

The Chaplain and the Methodist ministers, Dr. Robb and Dr. Speed, have all continued to give us their unfailing help and friendship, and we would like to take this opportunity of saying "thank you" to them, and to all our other friends, too numerous to mention by name, for all the kindness shown to us throughout the year.

APRIL 1ST 1950 TO MARCH 31ST 1951

This year 59 girls and 40 babies were dealt with: 31 girls went home or to friends, 7 to situations, 4 to other homes and 17 remained in the Home; 25 babies were kept with their mothers, 8 were adopted, 5 went to nurseries and 2 died. Miss Ackroyd's report continued:

By comparing this year's report with that of 1949-50, you will see that we have helped about the same number of girls each year, but the problems which confront us, though somewhat alike in essence, are very varied and each requires vastly different treatment.

One of the disappointing features, is the number of girls coming to us from homes of a good standard, because whilst this gives us, perhaps, a greater opportunity of teaching, it also indicates very strongly the different standard of morals which exists today, and the lack of wise handling by the parents. It also makes the future of the girl and her baby's, a much more difficult problem.

1950-51 has been, in many ways, a very happy year in the working of the Home. Never before I think, have so many friends rallied around us, and done so much for us. It would be impossible to enumerate the actual gifts, or to express adequate thanks, but we are very conscious of all the kindness we have received.

We have had many visitors to the Home, thus extending the interest to an ever widening circle of people.

Many articles of equipment have been added, and by the generosity of the St. Agnes Branch of the British Legion, new curtains are in all the rooms, but there is still much needing to be done.

There have been some changes of staff, but we are fortunate in having now a really adequate and able staff, and we owe them a very real debt of gratitude.

Special thanks must be given to our Chaplain, the Rev. G.H. Barnicoat, to the Methodist Minister, the Rev. F. White, and to our doctors for their unfailing help and friendship; and not least to the house committee for their understanding help.

APRIL 1ST 1951 TO MARCH 31ST 1952

Annual report missing from the records.

APRIL 1ST 1952 TO MARCH 31ST 1953

The figures for the year: 70 girls and 46 babies dealt with; 38 girls went home or to friends, 5 to situations, 4 to other homes; 23 were still in the Home; 24 mothers kept their babies, 14 were adopted, 7 were transferred to nurseries and 1 died. Miss Ackroyd reported:

> This has been a year of steady, quiet progress, without very much change in the usual pattern of events. We have had our disappointments when we have felt that we were working against innumerable [sic] odds, but we have also had our very happy times when we could see definite signs of progress in those for whom we are caring.
>
> The work is changing slowly, both in the type of girls who come to us and in particular in their attitude towards the kind of help offered, and in their attitude towards their responsibilities.

It is encouraging to find that although the present day tendency is to refuse to accept any discipline or restraint, there are still those who feel their responsibilities so keenly that they are prepared to accept the discipline of six months in a home such as ours, and there are many who write to us after they have left the Home, expressing their appreciation, and saying that it is only after they have left, that they have realised to the full, all that the influence of the Home has meant to them.

It is interesting, and rather sad to notice the change that comes over most of the girls during the last few weeks before they leave us, when they begin to realise that they are going to take up the threads once more, and they will no longer have the protection of the Home, and it is at this time, during their first months of a more normal way of living, that our prayers are so much needed for them.

We are very grateful for all the help which has been given to us through the "Friends of Rosemundy," and all those others who are too many to mention individually.

Our Chaplain, the Rev. G.H. Barnicoat, the Methodist Minister, the Rev. F.A. White, Dr. Robb and Dr. Speed, together with many other people, have all been unfailing in their generous help and sympathy.

We are in the happy position of having a most helpful and regular Committee, and we owe a great debt of gratitude to them, as well as to our loyal and hardworking staff.

APRIL 1ST 1953 TO MARCH 31ST 1954

This year 77 girls and 51 babies were dealt with; 46 girls went home or to friends, 4 to situations, 4 to other homes and 23 remained in the Home; 27 babies were kept with their mothers, 13 went to adopting parents, 5 to nurseries and 6 were still in the Home. Miss Ackroyd submitted her annual report:

This has been a somewhat difficult year, with changes of staff and several ups and downs, but we have also been able to do a good deal of steady progressive work.

We have had to turn down a good many applications for beds and it shows only too clearly the great need for the continuance of a Home such as this.

One very encouraging feature is the number of girls who keep their babies and do their best to care for and look after them.

Top left: Miss Barbara Ackroyd with a baby in the early 1950s. *Top right:* Midwife Nurse Waite.
Above: Rosemundy House in 1953.

It is becoming increasingly difficult to cope with the entire lack of responsibility to be found in the girls who come to our Homes, and in view of the material needs which seem to be provided so freely for them it is not easy for them to realise that work and responsibility are an essential part of everyday life. At the same time it is good to see how many do respond to the teaching and training we are able to give them.

We have had several highlights during the year, to which we look back with pleasure. One of these was the Outing given to the girls at the time of the Coronation. Another was the very reverent performance of the Nativity Tableaux to which we were able to welcome so many of our friends.

After Christmas a Choir from Stenalees came and sang carols for and with us and gave us all much pleasure.

We have had several visits from parties of people and this is a valuable means of spreading a knowledge and sympathy towards the work.

We acknowledge with sincere gratitude the debt we owe to the "Friends of Rosemundy," under the chairmanship of Mrs. Asher, J.P. The amount they do for us is almost incredible and both by their efforts and the help of the Council we have been able to equip the Home more efficiently.

I should like to express my gratitude to all those who continue to help us year by year: the Vicar and the Methodist Minister, Dr. Robb, Dr. Speed, and Dr. Smith, our own Home Committee, which is unfailing in its help and backing, to Miss Houghton, and last, but by no means least, I should like to thank Miss Jones for all the help she gives to the Home voluntarily and in her free time, and the Staff who work extremely hard, often under trying circumstances and are so very loyal to the Home and all it stands for.

APRIL 1ST 1954 TO MARCH 31ST 1955

Annual report missing from the records.

APRIL 1ST 1955 TO MARCH 31ST 1956

Annual report missing from the records.

APRIL 1ST 1956 TO MARCH 31ST 1957

During the year there were 50 girls and 34 babies in the Home; 21 of the mothers were Cornish girls, 8 were living or working in Cornwall and 21 were from other counties; 13 babies remained with their mothers, 19 were adopted and 2 went to homes or nurseries supported by mothers; 15 girls remained in the Home. The annual report continued:

> The Friends of Rosemundy organised a Garden Fete in July, which was successful and well attended in lovely weather, and a Presentation and farewell Party for Miss Ackroyd and Miss Jones on September 8th.
>
> Miss Launchbury took up her new duties as Matron on September 15th and has been given a warm welcome.
>
> The staff has been reduced by one, there is now no House Matron and, at present, only a daily Kitchen Matron.
>
> Plans are now in hand for demolishing part of the back premises and outbuildings which have proved to be in a dangerous condition and, owing to the lack of finances, no new building is possible to replace the

Presentation at the farewell party for Miss Ackroyd.

dormitory space lost by this. The maternity department is also involved, but by reducing the capacity of the Home from 24 to 15, plus the staff, it is proposed to rearrange the accommodation in the main part of the house, with some alterations, to enable the work to carry on as before.

APRIL 1ST 1957 TO MARCH 31ST 1958

Annual report missing from the records.

APRIL 1ST 1958 TO MARCH 31ST 1959

There were 11 girls and 8 babies in the Home at the beginning of the year, and since then admissions were: 52 girls aged 14-28; 33 babies. In the Home at the end of the year, 14 girls and 4 babies. Nine babies returned home with their mothers, 15 were adopted, 2 remained with their mothers in residential employment, 2 were taken into the care of the local authority, 1 died and 1 was stillborn. The report continued:

> The girls in the Home have come from many and varied walks of life. They have been school teachers, nurses, hotel workers, typists, shop assistants, domestic workers and schoolgirls, and the main age group seems to have been 17-21. They have not all come from Cornwall, although preference is always given to Cornish cases when there is limited accommodation.
>
> The new scheme of having the midwifery in the Home carried out entirely by the District Midwives is working out very happily, and thanks and appreciation must be expressed to the Nurses concerned for their care and kindness in the Maternity section of Rosemundy Home.
>
> The repairs and renovations so far completed in the Home have improved conditions considerably, and television (installed in time for Christmas) has given much pleasure to the girls.
>
> Thanks are due to the Home Committee, and the Garden Fete Committee and many others who do so much to help and encourage the Matron and help the Home; with them must be included the three Chaplains who undertake the spiritual care of those who come into our care in Rosemundy Home.

Miss Launchbury has had a difficult year with shortage and illness of staff, and more adequate staffing is still needed (if suitable applicants could be found for this specialised type of work) but she has emerged from it with her characteristic quality of cheerfulness and spiritual buoyancy, and many parents have cause to thank her for her motherly care of their girls.

APRIL 1ST 1959 TO MARCH 31ST 1960

Annual report:

There were 14 girls and four babies in the Home at the beginning of the year, and since then the numbers have been:– 57 girls, 50 babies born … In the Home at the end of the year, 14 girls and eight babies. Ages have ranged from 14-28, and the average age of the girls has been 16-20. Further repairs and redecoration have greatly improved the appearance of the Home, and a small legacy has made possible the purchase of a Spin Dryer for the laundry.

In common with most Homes in the country there is still difficulty in obtaining adequate staff of the right type for Rosemundy. Residential work is not popular in these days, since there are so many jobs available with shorter hours and larger wages.

The Fete Committee and Flora Dance Committee have given their usual kind help and support with annual events.

There have been gifts and appreciative letters from girls (and their parents) who have been helped in the Home, and it is very obvious that many who come from broken homes and whose lives have had no stability have learned to value the security of Rosemundy Home.

We are glad that Miss Launchbury has made a safe and speedy recovery from appendicitis.

APRIL 1ST 1960 TO MARCH 31ST 1961

The annual report indicated that there were 14 girls and 8 babies in the Home on the 1st April 1960; 59 girls were admitted between the 1st April 1960 and the 31st March 1961, and 45 babies were born during that period. Still in the Home on the 31st March 1961 were 17 girls and 4 babies. The report continued:

> Of the 59 girls mentioned, 27 were Cornish girls, 6 working in Cornwall, 26 from other Counties.

> The Home has had great difficulty in finding permanent resident staff, and a great strain has been placed on those who have to bear the daily burdens of a Home of this size and type.

> We are grateful to Miss Warwicker, and Mrs. Gowland for their very kind help during holidays and sickness.

> The Home has benefitted from various money raising efforts, Jumble Sales, Flora Dances, the summer Garden Fete, all very well supported, and thanks are due to the organizers.

> The programme of necessary repairs, re-decoration and renewals is progressing well, and with the drive to the Home re-surfaced, both the approach to the house and the house itself are very pleasing.

APRIL 1ST 1961 TO MARCH 31ST 1962

In the Home on the 1st April 1961 there were 17 girls and 4 babies; 54 girls were admitted between that date and the 31st March 1962, and 37 babies were born during the year. In the Home at the end of this period were 12 girls and 4 babies; of the 54 admissions, 27 were Cornish residents, 7 were working in Cornwall and 20 were from other counties; of the babies, 18 were placed with a view to adoption, 11 remained with their own mothers, 1 was placed with a foster mother and 3 were stillborn. The report went on:

> The ages of the girls varied from 14 to 19. A home teacher has visited the Home to enable any girls of school age to continue with their education while resident there.

> Miss Beaudet has been welcomed as a new member of the staff, working on the Nursery and Maternity side, and has shown herself to be a cheerful and capable helper.

New linoleum has greatly improved the appearance of a number of rooms in the Home. The Annual Meeting of the Association was held last December at Rosemundy, when many friends and supporters were welcomed, and much new interest has developed since.

The local Churches united and arranged a very successful and happy At Home, with Bring and Buy Sale in the Home before Christmas, and thanks are expressed to all concerned.

The Annual Garden Fete was held in the summer, thanks to the hard work and efforts of the Fete Committee under the leadership of Major Watton, and with the very capable help of Mrs. Stowell, whose passing has since been sadly recorded.

APRIL 1ST 1962 TO MARCH 31ST 1963

The annual report:

Resident in the Home on 1st April 1962, 12 girls and 4 babies. Admitted between April 1st 1962 and March 31st 1963, 65 girls and 45 babies. In the Home at the end of the year to which this report relates, 16 girls and 9 babies. Of the total number of admissions – 41 were Cornish Girls, 2 were working in Cornwall, 22 were from other counties.

[Of the] babies 28 were placed with a view to adoption, 14 remained with their mothers, 3 were placed with foster mothers, 2 were still-born, 1 died in Hospital. Three girls married the fathers of their babies.

The members of staff in the Home have remained the same during the past year and appreciation is expressed for their loyal service.

The usual Garden Fete organised by the kind friends of the Fete Committee was held in June, with fine weather to add to its success.

Members of the Church of England Men's Society from the Royal Naval Air Station at Culdrose, under the leadership of their Chaplain have kindly helped with some gardening on Saturday afternoons, and have made the kind gift of a new metal wheel-barrow for use in the garden. Gratitude is expressed also for gifts of cushions, baby clothes, and Harvest Festival fruit and vegetables from various friends and supporters.

A survey has been carried out at Rosemundy Home, with a view to long term planning and improvement of equipment and amenities, including some form of central heating.

APRIL 1ST 1963 TO CLOSURE OF HOME (OCTOBER 1964)

Report(s) missing.

A NURSE REMEMBERS

In 1951 Margaret Smith went to work at the Home as a nurse. At this time Miss Ackroyd was the Lady Superintendent. Margaret worked there until 1959, and in 2007 she wrote to the author with information about the Home and her time there:

I was there from 1951 to 1959 and was in charge of mothers and babies from fourteen days. The ages of the mothers ranged from fourteen to thirty years and were mostly from the West Country and they stayed for six or more weeks after delivery. When I arrived the home was paid for by the Moral Welfare Association but after I left it was handed over to the County Council.

Miss Knell was House Matron, Mrs Tre Smith helped in the nursery. The cook was Miss Wroughton followed by Mrs Pharaoh. Mrs Ramsey was the Laundry Matron. My jobs were many, up at 5.30am, call mothers and make them all tea, supervise 6am feed, wash bottles and teats. Breakfast was at 8.00, followed by a service in the Chapel. Then it was bathing time and 10am feed. I was teaching them all how to care for their babies.

It was a very happy home. I am afraid some of the people in St Agnes Church thought we spoiled them. But I had an answer, there but for the grace of God

Nurse Smith at Rosemundy in the 1950s.

go I. Also the man goes off and the poor girl is left to carry the baby and go through a painful labour with no support. Some mothers as young as 14 years, only a child themselves.

Our matrons had no medical knowledge. They were just trained in Moral Welfare, like our social workers today. So when our midwife left I had a big responsibility.

My other jobs included caring for our Chapel, preparing it for Holy Communion on Tuesday mornings at 7am. This was taken by my father. One or two members of the Church regularly attended.

I organised social events for the girls, the Christmas party etc. We had no night nurse so I looked after all the babies at night. My room was next to the nursery. I also helped with deliveries.

When I started work there, we took in 24 girls. In about 1957 it was discovered that the labour ward and one dormitory was in danger of collapsing. A meeting of the general committee was summoned which included the Medical Officer of Health, Dr Curnow. It was decided to pull those rooms down, as it was a cheaper option. This meant the home had just room to take in 15 girls. Sadly our midwife had to leave as there wasn't enough work to keep her employed. This of course gave me a great deal more responsibility.

While the work was carried out the girls had to be delivered at Redruth Hospital, and then returned to us.

When we were all straight again the district nurses came in to do the deliveries and the antenatal clinic once a week. The girls would come to me day or night if they started in labour or felt unwell. I would decide when to call the nurse. At night I always got up and put my uniform on so I could be with the girl to give her assurance and support.

The girls all had jobs to do in the home, supervised by Miss Knell. Cleaning of dormitories, helping in the kitchen and laundry. Mrs Ramsay the Laundry Matron came in on Mondays and Wednesdays. The coppers had to be filled and the fires lit before breakfast. We had no central heating. A stove in the dining room heated the water. The nursery was heated by way of one bar electric fires from the ceiling. The girls' sitting room and the staff room all had open fires.

The girls could go out into the village in the afternoons. They just had to tell us they were going so we knew where they were in case any visitors came.

On Wednesday afternoons they could go to the Regal Cinema, so after dinner I would say, "How many for the cinema, hands up?" Then I would ring Mr Taylor, give him the numbers and he would reserve seats for them, charging them sixpence each.

On arrival at the home they would be interviewed by the matron being asked their religion, among other things. Church of England girls would be taken to the 11am Mass on Sundays either by me or the midwife. The Methodists would go to the Chapel & one of the members would look after them. Likewise the Roman Catholics.

On Thursday afternoons the Methodist Minister would talk to the Chapel girls in the Chapel in the home. There would be a hymn, bible reading and prayers. Afterwards he would join all the girls in their sitting room over a cup of tea.

On Friday afternoons Father Barnicoat would do the same with the Church of England girls. The Roman Catholic girls who were usually just one or two would go out to tea once a week with a member of the Church. I don't remember her name.

Those girls who were keeping their babies and wished to have them baptised before leaving the home had a choice. They could either have a baptism in the Church or Chapel or in our own Chapel. Most chose our Chapel. Then it was my job to contact the Vicar or Methodist Minister to arrange a day and time.

All the girls & Matron would come to the service. I had one gown which was worn by all babies baptised. After each one I would wash it and iron it and keep it in my special cupboard of baby clothes.

All expectant mothers, a month before they were due to have their babe, I would give them a bundle and go through it with them. Each one would have nappies, cot sheets, blankets, matinee coats and bootees and mittens. They then had to sign for them. I was then able to check I had the same number of clothes when they left. All the mothers from 14 days washed their own baby clothes. Mrs Ramsey would boil nappies on Mondays and Wednesdays.

Before the mothers left us they had to provide a set of clothes for their babies. Many evenings I have spent in the girls' sitting room teaching some to knit.

I had one whole day off a week. The few hours each day were often disturbed unless I went out. But it never worried me as any of the girls knew that I was always ready to listen to their problems. I did my best to be a mother to them all.

Our medical officer was Dr Robb of Perranporth. He or one of his partners came over once a week for an antenatal clinic and to do a medical on any of my babies due to leave. Also I was able to let him see any problems I had with any of the others. They also looked after the staff.

Refurbished chapel in 1956.

Father Barnicoat

The girls went to Mr Batten the dentist in the village. When he left we had to take them to Mr Gunlack at Perranporth.

In the grounds of Rosemundy there was a small bungalow. This was the home of Miss Jones, followed by Miss Proctor. They were the outdoor workers. They would go and visit the girls prior to them coming to the home.

The busiest time of the year was Christmas. No decorations were put up until Christmas Eve. It was then all go! Miss Collette always gave us a large tree for the hall. It took a good while to decorate. We would give the girls a box of decorations and let them decorate their own sitting room. They were not allowed to stand on chairs or climb ladders. I had a small tree with lights in the nursery and Nurse Waite would put one in the lying-in room. A nativity scene which had been made of wood and painted by Margaret Truscott, was erected on the outdoor stage. Percy James fixed lights on the tree to the right of the front door. I put our little crib up in the Chapel. It was now lunch time. After the 2pm feed I spent the afternoon in the kitchen making things for the party. Then it was thinking up games, wrapping prizes. Later on I made up a little stocking for each baby. I knitted them all a pair of bootees and a pair of mittens and added a bar of soap. All the girls had a present.

Later on Mrs Tre Smith would make pasties for everyone for supper. Then about 7pm Father Barnicoat would come down and bless our crib and we would sing carols around our tree.

I gave myself an hour of quiet to get ready for midnight mass. I left the midwife babysitting.

On Christmas Day I was up as usual at 5.30am. Then at 6am we were all woken up by the Chapel Choir and St Agnes Band singing carols outside the front door.

After the 10am feed I took the girls to Church. Then it was back to Christmas lunch. The staff all waited on the girls. We also did all the washing up.

The afternoon I spent preparing for the party, laying a table for the buffet supper. At 9.30pm we listened to carols on Miss Jones' gramophone and had our evening prayers. Then it was goodnight to expectant mums and feeding time for babies. A good many mothers said it was the best Christmas they had ever had.

Miss Knell, our house matron, was a twin to Bishop Knell, Bishop of Reading. I suggested to Miss Knell if she would help me in sprucing up the chapel. I consulted Miss Ackroyd who agreed if we could find the money. We had jumble sales, coffee mornings etc. When we had enough we painted the walls. Mr Reynolds did the ceiling for us free of charge. We made new curtains, bought new chairs. Miss Jones found a second-hand harmonium. My mother gave us two glass vases for the altar. I asked the Vicar if we could have it dedicated. He said, "Leave it all with me; I will get in touch with the Bishop."

We had a lovely service. As we were unable to fit everyone into the Chapel, we had a large marquee erected on the lawn and the service was relayed outside. Afterwards we served refreshments.

Later on Bishop Knell came and spent the week-end with us. He asked me if we had any vestments. I said, "No, my father celebrated in cassock and surplice." The next thing I knew he presented us with an amice, alb, cincture, stole and a green chasuble.

I turned the small room which wasn't used into a vestry. This room was right next to the Chapel.

We held a large fete in the summer on the lawn, or if wet indoors. All the organizations in the village had a stall. We also had a staff stall helped by our mothers. My mother always came down and helped with refreshments. It was a very big event with an opener and everybody dressed in their summer best. A good many women wore summer hats. No trousers or jeans were seen on any females.

As well as the fete, the Garden Theatre Players put on performances in the summer. One year we had the Ballet Minerva. They camped in the grounds with tents for the men and caravans for the women. They used our bathrooms. We also had, as now, floral dances.

THE REVEREND JOE RIDHOLLS

ST AGNES METHODIST MINISTER

I was the Methodist minister in St Agnes from 1957 to 1962. I am in no position to comment on the alleged conditions at the home, or the life of the girls, but I feel things need saying. Views were very different in those days and Rosemundy met a need, making provisions for girls who found themselves in a very difficult situation. I did hear talk once of 'that type of girl' but there was no 'type'. They came from a variety of backgrounds but were all very needy.

I often thought of the words of Robbie Burns: *'Ye high, exalted, virtuous dames, tied up in godly laces, before ye gie poor Frailty names, suppose a change o' cases. A dear lov'd lad, convenience snug, a treacherous inclination – but let me whisper i' your lug, Ye're aiblins [maybe] nae temptation!'*

Predecessors of mine used faithfully to visit the home and talk to the girls. My wife would invite them into our home, two or three at a time, for a cup of tea and homemade cakes. Joan also knitted various garments for their babies.

Revd Joe Ridholls with his wife Joan and young family.

MOTHERS

During the research for this book many mothers contacted the writer to give memories of their time spent at Rosemundy House. Some have been recorded in full in the book; others wish to remain totally anonymous with just some of their memories recorded. The mothers who have made contact were all at Rosemundy in the post-War period so it is not clear how mothers felt about the Home before this time. When the Home was first opened, mothers stayed for nine months after the birth of their baby, but by the 1950s mothers stayed a shorter time after birth – about 8 weeks if the baby was adopted and 6 months if they were keeping the child.

It is difficult to generalise about life in the Home because the regime would have changed at different times, and each Matron had her own way of running it.

It does however seem likely that it has always been a frightening experience for the mothers-to-be, arriving at this large house and not knowing what was waiting for them inside. Most were to find life at the Home very hard and unpleasant, but a few thought that it was not too bad and were reasonably happy there.

The first procedure following arrival was usually an interview with the Matron in her office (the first room on the left upon entering the front door).

The day started with breakfast, and one of girls would help to prepare it. This was usually cereal and toast. The girls had work to do during the morning: cleaning, dusting, scrubbing floors, working in the garden, polishing the brass in the Matron's office and (what most mothers hated) working in the laundry room. Here all washing was done in a cauldron – a fire had to be lit under it, and dirty nappies, bed linen, sheets from the labour ward and staff clothes had to be washed. Ironing was done with old fashioned flat-irons. Lunch was followed by a free afternoon when the girls could go for a walk; some went as far as Perranporth. One afternoon a week they could go to the Regal Cinema in St Agnes but always had to be back in time for tea. The evenings were spent in the lounge which was always cold, though there was a fire. Wood had to be collected from the woods in the grounds. Some mothers would steal coal from under the stairs, which was there for the roaring fire in the Matron's office. During the evening the girls would chat, knit, read or listen to the radio. By Christmas 1958 there was even a television.

Before going to bed mothers would go to the chapel for a blessing and a prayer for their babies.

Two mothers, at the Home in 1956, sent the writer these words to the Babies' Prayer:

> We thank you for the safe delivery of Mother and Baby (names),
> God bless the babies in this home,
> That they may grow up patient and kind,
> To become God's faithful soldiers and servants,
> Until their lives end.

MOTHERS REMEMBER

RENE

ROSEMUNDY 1948

Before going to Rosemundy I was taken by a social worker to a place in Penzance as there was no room at Rosemundy. I don't know how the social worker became involved unless my doctor contacted her. After a short time I was taken to Rosemundy. This was in March 1948, three months before my daughter Shirley was born. I don't remember much about arriving there as I was very upset, leaving home for the first time and being very close to my mum and knowing she would have had me at home if she had the room. I was 19 when I had my baby in the June and I stayed for three months after her birth, leaving in September 1948. Sister Rowe the midwife delivered my baby and Miss Ackroyd was there as well. Miss Ackroyd was the matron and she was lovely. She told me that if I was not able to take my baby home she would find a place where I could work with Shirley. I was not aware of any mothers being made or pressured to have their babies adopted.

Before my baby was born I lived in the main house but moved to the Long Room outside once she was born. At night we put our babies to bed in the nursery after we had fed them. In the morning we would go to the nursery and pick them up and feed them and on nice days we would put them out in prams on the lawn. As I remember we were not stopped from seeing our babies because when my mother came to see me and my baby was only a few days old, I took her to the nursery to see her.

We all had jobs to do during the day but I didn't mind – someone had to do them. If our job needed afternoon or evening work we would do it; for instance, when I was on the boiler it had to be stoked up for the night.

Food was adequate, we were never hungry; we sat at a long table for meals, I did however hate the macaroni cheese. In 1948 there was still rationing and all the mothers had their own sugar which was kept in cocoa tins painted orange; mine had the number 23 on it.

On arrival we were asked what religion we were. I was Methodist but told them I was Church of England and attended the Church in St Agnes every Sunday. There was also a small chapel in Rosemundy House and we had a service there every week and a vicar or minister would come in.

On the lawn there was a chalet where the prams were kept and we would put our babies in them on the lawn on nice days.

At Christmas, after I left, Miss Ackroyd sent me a Christmas card.

Left: Rene with her daughter Shirley (front row, right). *Right, l-r:* Rene with Shirley, Sister Rowe the midwife with two babies and another mother with her baby. In the background is the shelter in the garden where the prams were stored.

Grant us, O Lord, to know that which is worth knowing, to love that which is worth loving, to praise that which pleaseth Thee most, to esteem that highly which to Thee is precious, and to abhor that which in Thy sight is contemptible. We ask all this for Thy Name's Sake. Amen.

Thomas à Kempis

The Chapel,
Rosemundy,
St. Agnes.

With love to you both
for Christmas
from
B. Ackroyd

GREETINGS

Christmas card from Miss Ackroyd to Rene.

PEGGY

ROSEMUNDY 1952

I arrived at Rosemundy on the 1st March 1952 and left on the 1st of September; my baby was born on the 4th June. I was 19 when I arrived and the same age when my son was born. There were 23 mothers in the Home when I was there.

It was very strict there and not much food. A treat was a piece of fried bread on Sundays. Breakfast was dry bread with no butter just marmalade. One girl would pick up the remains of the dried bread and eat during the day. Every week we had a different job, the laundry, kitchen garden and sweeping leaves in the wood. We had to saw wood in the stables using a two-person saw. The wood came from the woods or farmers would drop some off. We had to make babies' cot mattresses using straw in the stable. It looked like old packing straw and full of glass, we had to pick it all out and put it in the mattresses. Once a week we went to the minister's house for tea, the Rev. White; we also went to Chapel, they treated us really well. In the evenings we went to the chapel in the Home.

We were not allowed to take our babies away from the Home, babies were put in prams in the summerhouse on the grass and sister and the midwife would look after them. I only saw my baby every four hours when I fed him, I breast fed him for 3 months. The day started with a 6am feed, 9am bath, then 10am, 2pm, 6pm and 10pm feeds. After the 2pm feed we could go out but had to be back by 5pm, occasionally we went to the cinema in the village.

I remember one girl went out in the afternoon and met a man in a car, she was still pregnant and he was probably the father of her child. The Home found out about it and threw her out. She packed her bags and left. I often think about her.

Prior to the adoption handover we went to the nursery and were given a second hand case of clothes. I acquired a new romper suit for him and didn't use the clothes in the case. I spent an hour getting him ready then matron came and took him. I looked out of the nursery window and saw a man and woman taking him down the drive. After my baby had been taken my parents came to fetch me after dark. I didn't want to go, especially without my baby. I had been happy at the home. My parents said, "That's it now, gone and forgotten". I left with two little photos of my baby taken by a friend at the home. My mother found them one day and showed them to my father who tore them up and put them on the fire.

VIOLET

ROSEMUNDY 1953

I was allowed to spend my last Christmas and New Year at home with my family. It was 1952 and was the last time we were going to be together. On the second of January 1953 I was taken to Rosemundy House, a home for unmarried women. I was pregnant with my beautiful daughter. Miss Ackroyd and Miss Jones were in charge (Matrons) and Sister Bath was my midwife. She was good to me. I had to be taken to my bed as I had high blood pressure and toxaemia. I was in bed for three weeks. Sister Bath came to me and said Miss Ackroyd wanted to see me right away. I was told my Dad had died. It was February 1953 and he was 62 years old.

Someone took me to Stratton to see my mother and family. I wasn't allowed to go and see my Dad and had to go back to Rosemundy. I wasn't allowed to go to his funeral because of my condition. Anyway, I was 15 years old on the 1st April 1953 and 3rd April was Good Friday. On Monday 6th April I wasn't feeling very well and told Sister Bath. She examined me and she said I could be in early stages of labour. Next I was given a job to do. I had to scrub all the polish off the upstairs landing then wait for it to dry. Then I put polish back on and had to buff it till it shone. It took me all day except for breaks for lunch and dinner. In the evening we had a beetle drive. Half way through I couldn't bear it anymore. Sister Bath took me up to delivery room, it took 2½ hours for my lovely daughter to be born. It was love at first sight. She was lovely, she was mine. 9lbs and three quarters in weight and now my life had a meaning. I had my little girl to look after. I breast fed her and I had enough milk to express for other babies. Life wasn't a bed of roses as I still had to help in kitchen and other jobs.

Some of the girls were nice to me but some were not so good – could've been because I was so young. Anyway, at 10 clock, I would have to feed Dulcie and top and tail her and put her to bed and go to dormitory and go to sleep myself. Every night I was told Dulcie is awake and hungry she needs feeding and nappy changed. It was always between eleven and eleven thirty. I would go down and the staff would say, 'This is what it's going to be like for the next five years. Why don't you let us adopt her? We have a lovely couple who would love to have her.' I would reply, 'I don't care, she is all mine and I don't care what or where I go, she goes with me.' In the end I was having nightmares. A doctor, I think he was called Dr Smith, told them to leave me alone.

We all had to stay at Rosemundy for six months. If you had your baby when you came there first you still had to stay six months. One young girl had her baby [at the beginning of her stay] and she had to bath and dress her baby. It was a little boy and she had to kiss him goodbye. He was about five months old and she had to leave him in his cot and go with her Mum and Dad. Her Dad said she had to get him adopted, it wasn't coming home with them.

So you see that made up my mind all the more. No one was doing that to me and my baby. Also, when we were giving our babies away, we had to leave them in the nursery in their cots, not on the lawns in prams. Things may have changed in 1959. Also each week we were rationed with our butter and margarine. One week we would have 1oz marg and 1oz butter. The following week it would be marg and it had to last. If someone took it, tough, you wouldn't have any more. I can remember I didn't know what a banana or an orange was, more so a banana.

When my time came to leave I had no choice because I was keeping my baby. I had to go to a children's home called Trelyn in Perranporth. There life was no better as I had all the dirty jobs to do. I stayed there until I met my first husband, but had to get permission to get married and he took Dulcie as his own. We both had to adopt my daughter. My daughter has given me 1 granddaughter, 2 grandsons, 2 great-grandsons and 1 great-granddaughter.

PAT

ROSEMUNDY 1953-1954

My son was born in February 1954. I can't remember when I went there, it must have been before the Christmas. I was happy there, as an expectant mum we were put on light duties, like tidying the flower beds, bedrooms etc. When I was in matron's office there were no vacuums, we had to use dust pan and brush. As a new mum it was washing and ironing and other light duties, a strong mum it was shovelling coal and other heavy duties. Our time there was about six months unless the babies were adopted. We were allowed to go to the pictures, in a group supervised and put over in the far side away from other people so as not to corrupt the young lads of the village. There was a lady who lived in the village who was in charge of the kitchen, we called her aunt something, I can't remember. I was at the home for my 21st birthday and they laid on a special tea that day with a cake.

They were strict but in those days we were considered naughty girls, not like today.

When we were out of bed for the first time we were allowed down the main staircase just the once, then it was the back stairs. We went to church on Sundays, my son was christened there, they supplied a long christening gown and the midwife was godmother.

When a baby was born we had a service in the Home's chapel to welcome the new baby.

So in my opinion I was happy there and I didn't regret keeping my son. Twelve years later my son had a best friend at school and he turned out to be born at the same time but was adopted by a couple in Jersey.

LYN

ROSEMUNDY 1956

1956 was a year that I will never ever forget. That was the year that I was going to get married to my then fiancée, but after a lot of rows and pretend heart attacks from my future Mother-in-law, I walked away and left Mother and Son to get on with their lives without me and the baby I was expecting.

This meant that I would be going to Rosemundy House in St Agnes to have the baby with the knowledge that it would have to be adopted when born as in those times there was not the help for single Mums as there is nowadays.

So bags packed I made my way to Rosemundy – I had no idea what was to come in the future there, I was not expecting a holiday camp but also I was not prepared for Rosemundy and its regime.

Rules and more rules, break them at your peril, the impression one got was that you had committed the worst sin in the world and YOU were going to pay!

The food was adequate but awful, and this was the place where you learned what work was and how hard it would be. Everyone was issued with a list of jobs to be completed for the day and the only way to be excused from them was to go into labour. The job everyone hated was the Laundry with the huge coppers where all the linen was plunged and then boiled. Rinsed and rinsed then put through the mangles. Scrubbing floors on your knees was a doddle compared to the Laundry! The heat and steam there was awful, health and safety would never stand for it today!

You did get chances to go to the Village to either shop or just stroll around, but there again there were limits that you were allowed to go to; some of the Villagers just could not accept that you weren't in their village from choice and they would openly and very loudly say what they thought of you and your "bump". It was horrible the first time you encountered this attitude but after a while you learned to put it down to ignorance and sometimes would retaliate with remarks like "There but for the grace of God go you – perhaps?" but there was the other side of the village and the people who would stop and ask you how you were getting along, some of the shopkeepers would give Rosemundy girls a bit of discount or some small freebies. We had to attend Church or Chapel on Sundays and then be back at Rosemundy in time for visitors – if you were lucky to get some. The inmates were all very good to each other if one had visitors and someone else had none, the lucky ones would share their company, no one was ever left alone.

We were allowed to attend the village Cinema sometimes and there one could have a frightening experience, usually about halfway through the film something would suddenly land on your lap – the local cat!

The resident Midwife (Nurse Waite) was very strict but I found that she would listen to your troubles and would always try to help or give advice where she could, other members of the Staff were quite the opposite and lived by the saying "You made your bed – now get on with it".

The worst part of this whole episode in my life was when I had to take my 6 week old son to Bath to the adoption agency, there to hand him over to the new parents.

You were given your rail ticket, a bag to carry baby's belongings and feeds, you were then driven to the station and after that you were on your own.

I arrived at the office – what a bleak place that was!

Bare wooden floorboards and hard chairs in the waiting room and a hard faced receptionist behind the desk.

All you got from her was "Name and baby's name". Then she disappeared into the next room, you could hear voices but not what was being said, then she re-entered and asked you to sign the paperwork that she just thrust in front of you and she took my son into the next room, she came back again alone, and said, "You can go now – if you hurry you will catch the return train to Cornwall". (She held the door open to make sure you were leaving and said) "Goodbye!" and then the door slammed behind you.

And that was that – not an ounce of feeling or care from her, she was just doing a job!!!

I cried all the way back to St Agnes, and I had to stay there for a few days until everything was settled, it was awful after leaving your baby behind and going back to all the other Mums and their babies. If they were lucky they would not have to go through that experience as a lot of prospective parents collected their new family from Rosemundy.

You always knew when prospective parents were due to view because all the babies were placed in their prams all clean and spruced up ready for the inspection and all the Mums were sent to the dormitory and we had to stay there until we were told we could come out again and all visitors had gone.

50 years later my son managed to trace me, we met and we have been in regular contact ever since, he told me that I had 3 Grandchildren and since that meeting my Grandson has married and now he has a lovely little boy of his own so now I am a Great-grandma.

I was lucky that my son was adopted by excellent parents who could give him all the things in life that I would never had been able to give him, and I appreciate their guidance for him; others who were adopted were not so lucky with their lives and parents.

LYN RODDEN (FORMERLY LINDA BURROUGHS)

The Secrets of Rosemundy House

IRIS

ROSEMUNDY 1956

My son was born at Rosemundy House on the 9th April 1956. My boyfriend, who I later married, was the father of the baby. Miss Ackroyd who ran the house was very strict but nurse Smith and nurse Waite were lovely.

The girls received a shilling a week pocket money but I didn't. My boyfriend phoned me every night and I was told if I stopped speaking to him I would get mine; I never got any. I found the food was good because we cooked it ourselves; a nurse stood over us making sure it was cooked right. I was never cold but was unhappy there and felt we were treated like prisoners. We had to scrub floors, do the washing and ironing and run the house. After lunch we were allowed to go out if we asked permission but had to wear green arm bands. On Sundays we walked to Church in twos.

I breast fed my baby and it was my intention to keep him, my boyfriend had done a mechanic's course but we had nowhere to live. There was no room at home, my grandmother had died and my mother lived with my grandfather. My son was Christened Robert and on leaving Rosemundy he went to Exeter Dr Barnardo's Home and we would visit him every Sunday. When he was nearly one we realised that we would not be able to keep him and it wasn't fair on him so we had him adopted. I have had no contact with him since this time.

JAN

ROSEMUNDY 1957

What a beautiful name for a home for young women who became pregnant, no pill at that time, no counselling, no benefits or in many cases no parents who were willing to look after their daughter who had brought shame to their home. So were sent to the "Homes" mainly run by the Church of England or to those run by the Catholic Church.

Rosemundy happened to be a Church of England "Home" – wasn't I the lucky one!

I suppose in many ways it wasn't quite so hard for me to settle into their harsh regime as I had just come out of the forces (WRNS). In those days if you became pregnant you had to leave so therefore I was used to being told what to do and where to go but most of the girls there at that time were of course completely fazed by all that was happening to them.

But I must go back to the beginning. It was the beginning of September, we arrived at this what I thought at the time a beautiful house, very old but well kept, manicured lawns but with baby prams on it and a lovely driveway leading to a large wooden door. I was escorted by two Wren Officers who I suppose thought that they were doing me a favour; I should have done a runner then and there if I had known what lay ahead of me; we were met by a rather small dour looking lady who told us that she was the matron. I was then taken upstairs using the grand staircase to my room which I was to share with 5 other "girls"; the Wren Officers at this time took their leave of me and I was left alone wondering what lay ahead of me; I was lucky because I had no problem with sharing as I had been used to dormitory life. The girls I shared this room with, their ages ranged from approx 14 yrs to one who was in her middle to late thirties, but of course this all kept changing; as "girls" had their babies they went and others came, but I was yet to experience all the trauma that went with this procedure.

After my two escorts left I was then told I must never again use the front staircase but had to use the back one, which I gathered had been the servants' stairway; I was then given the grand tour, told where to go and when for our meals!!, shown the labour room which to me at that time was the most frightening place I had ever seen, then on to the laundry room outside, where everyone had to do their washing, no washing machines in those days, everything had to be either hand washed or put into a large cauldron which was set into a brick oven type thing with a fire underneath which had to be lit and the water heated every Monday morning, guess whose job that was?!! But I really didn't mind that, as we had a local lady who used to come and help and supervise, maybe that is still why I enjoy washing and seeing everything nice and clean, but of course now I have all the mod cons, but back to Rosemundy again: everything had to be wrung out by hand and then the ironing – good old fashioned irons, not electric! We had of course, and it goes without saying, we had to do ALL the Staff's clothing.

At the time I was 5 months pregnant and still suffering from morning sickness which actually continued throughout my pregnancy; I was often in trouble about it, but no one cared or even thought to mention it to the doctor who came to visit approx once a month. I dare not mention it – if I had I would have caused problems for the midwife, and I certainly was not one of her favourite people, for what reason I never did know; her name I think was sister Wade.

As I said earlier it was quite a harsh regime, especially now when I see how pregnant women are treated and rightly so; they are cared for and monitored all through their pregnancy. I have two daughters and I must admit I certainly would not like them to have been treated as we were; unfortunately only one of my daughters has been able to have one child, and the one I kept (daughter) has not been able to have any children. Of course it has crossed my mind many times, was it through our ill treatment that something happened to her before she was born. I will never know and I have to live with that thought.

One of my strongest memories from that time was when it started to get cold in the evenings after we had all done our chores for the day, which could have been from washing and scrubbing the hard stone flagstone floors to polishing and cleaning the staff's private quarters, also collecting anything that could be useful to the members of the staff, making meals for them; the only meal they had with us was breakfast at 8am sharp, we actually had to make toast for the staff but could never have any ourselves until we had had our baby, and then it was only the crusts which had been cut off for them; our tea usually consisted of bread & jam and maybe a cake if one of the girls had been lucky enough to have had some money sent, but back to my memory: we all had to find wood and saw it up so we could have a fire in the evening to keep warm, otherwise we did not have any heat, but it was during those long cold Cornish winter evenings that we could be ourselves and be normal young women; I suppose looking back, those were the only happy times we had, but I do know that the only good thing that came out of all that was the friendship we all shared;

sadly we all eventually went our separate ways and those friendships are no more, is that good or bad? Maybe it was a time in our lives that we want to forget, but time for me has not healed the wounds.

Of course it was obligatory that we all had to attend the local church and were marched down every Sunday morning with all the locals looking and nodding away; some were nice and gave us nice smiles but OTHERS, well you just knew what they were thinking. I have driven down that road many times since and always that memory came back to haunt me; I can still hear the voice of the local vicar as he came twice a week to remind us of our SINS.

There are so many heart rending stories I could tell, from one girl running away and being brought back by the police and put into a small room alone and given very little food and drink for about a week. We had to try and sneak food to her; of course the larder was always locked and the matron guarded the key. Another who had her baby on a stone floor at the bottom of the servants' stairway by herself with no one to help or comfort her, again I still hear her screams and no one daring to move, but of course the saddest ones are the girls who were made to give up their babies; they had to look after their child for SIX WEEKS then feed and dress them in the layette as it was called then, put them in a pram in the garden and were then locked in their bedroom until the adoptive parents had been and collected the child. Every Saturday this happened and every Saturday there would be a heartbroken girl; those memories will live in my heart for ever, even after all these years when I read or see people who are looking for their son or daughter or vice versa. It still hurts, it was a real physical pain that those girls went through; it was after seeing this happen so many times I vowed it would not happen to me and although so much pressure was put on me to give my baby up for adoption, not only from the home but from my mother and the WRNS who were funding my stay there, I would not give my child away to strangers so it was not just the physical hardship that we went through, it was the mental one that did the most lasting damage to us all.

My time to have my baby came early one week exactly after my 21ˢᵗ birthday; I look back now and have to laugh, but at that time I was very frightened as my waters broke in the middle of the night. I remember thinking it was my water bottle that was leaking, but no, it was happening for me; I woke one of the girls up and she went for the midwife who then came and put me in a room on my own, saying, 'I will see you in the morning'; sure enough she arrived and said I had to go to the nearest hospital which happened to be Redruth (our labour ward was out of action). My little girl was born at 6.35 pm on the 30th Dec 1957. She of course was beautiful but so tiny; my resolution never wavered to give this child away, never!! Never!!

I eventually returned back to Rosemundy with her, but left four weeks later; my mother had relented and when she saw her first grandchild she wept, with joy; she became the absolute pride and joy to her and to me she became the most precious child, especially as she spent the second year of her life in hospital; she had actually been born with CDH (Congenital Dislocation of her Hips); it should have been discovered before we left Rosemundy by the doctor but never was. And now a woman who has given me and all her family such joy and love and continues to do so to her beloved husband and adopted son.

Throughout the years she has often asked me about her natural father; I have always been very honest with her and told her as much as she needed to be told. I myself married when she was 6 years old and so she has always regarded my husband as her father; we have also got two more children, another daughter and son; to them she is just their sister and Dad is Dad, but two years ago she said that she wanted to find her natural father; with a bit of luck and searching I found him and wrote to him telling him all about her and that she would like to have contact with him; he did reply to her and yes they did meet; he was surprised and delighted and of course now regrets that he did not fulfil his promises to me and her of course, but that is life, she is happy now and feels that all the gaps that had been missing in her life have now been filled.

Me, well Rosemundy and all my experiences there made me a stronger person and I have fulfilled all the promises that I made to myself whilst there. I consider I have been a very lucky lady; after Rosemundy I came home and went on to have a good career as a radiographer in a local hospital where I met my future husband and married a wonderful man; we have now been married for nearly 46 years, have three wonderful children and 4 grandchildren. As I said earlier my daughter has suffered badly with her health and continues to do so, but for all that she is one of the most compassionate people l know and I feel as though it all had to be and I was meant to give life to her and keep her close to my heart as I will, as long as I live.

MARJORY

ROSEMUNDY 1960

I was an evacuee from London to St Allen, aged two years and three months, in 1940. After the War my mother didn't want me back and I was brought up by my new parents, a priest and his wife, in Cornwall – I called the priest 'Father', his wife 'Mummy' and the housekeeper 'Aunt'. I was educated at home and was very naive. By the time I was 21 the priest and his wife had died and I was living with the housekeeper. I went a bit astray and became pregnant. The baby's father didn't know I was pregnant. I went to Rosemundy House to have my baby and he was born on the 4th April 1960 and weighed eight and a half pounds. I stayed at the Home for about 6 months. It was home from home. I had enough food and we were given small jobs; the girls, however, came from different backgrounds; many didn't take to work. Many girls were arrogant and had an attitude problem. We had to work but so what, we were grown women and didn't have modern appliances they have today. It was a tough regime but with caring staff. I can't criticise them. The hardest part was giving my son up when he was six weeks old. He was taken from me and I was told to go to one of the communal rooms and that was it; I heard no more of him.

VERONICA

ROSEMUNDY 1960

I lived in Budock Water but after I became pregnant I was ushered to an aunt at Totnes and then home for a fortnight before going to Rosemundy. I travelled to Rosemundy with a social worker and I remember feeling very scared, this was early July 1960 and I was only 16. On arrival at the Home I remember hearing the rooks in the trees and this will always remind me of Rosemundy. I was taken into the matron's office, a room on the left as you entered the house, and I remember she was a little fat lady. There were about 20 to 25 mothers there and I was nervous. I would sit in the large sitting room knitting, hoping that someone would chat and I could make friends. After just three weeks I went into labour, my waters broke but I didn't know what was happening, it was a very scary experience. On the 28th July my son was born weighing 5lb 10oz. A doctor was there at the time and nurse Stait. She was a lovely person; wonderful with babies and showed a lot of affection. After the birth I had a cold and was put into isolation. I didn't breast feed him and was given Epsom Salts to lose my milk. He took so long to bottle feed in the mornings I was often late for breakfast. After the birth he was to be adopted but because he was so tiny and difficult to feed this was delayed. The intention was for him to go to a Dr Barnardo's Home and be adopted from there. My mother would visit quite often and we would walk to the beach and the seal sanctuary, we would have endless arguments; I wanted to keep my baby, my parents wanted him to be adopted. I was eventually allowed to keep him and left the Home about eight weeks after the birth. My mother and father both adored my baby but my mother held it against me for the rest of her life.

ANN

ROSEMUNDY 1960–1961

When I was 18 I left my home at Newlyn to train as a nurse at Freedom Fields Hospital, Plymouth. I lived in the nurses' home and we were looked after by a sister. For 6 months while I was there I went out with a Chief Petty Officer from H.M.S. Raleigh called David. I attended many dances and dos at Raleigh with him. At the end of May 1960 I found I was pregnant and went to talk to him about it and in his office he had a photo of a lady and a baby that he said was his wife. I don't know if this was a borrowed photo or genuinely his family but that was it, I didn't see him again.

I carried on nursing and living in the nurses' home but I was gradually getting bigger and at 3-4 months was called in to ask if there was anything wrong. I must have been a bit stupid; my uniform was getting a bit tight. I had not told my parents but the hospital welfare did and my parents came to get me and I just disappeared from the hospital overnight. My parents were shocked, not for me: 'What would the neighbours think?' I couldn't go home to Newlyn and had to live with my gran at Buryas Bridge, in the shadows and out of the way. I didn't have a choice having no money, just hidden away. I stayed there until about the end of October when I was taken to Rosemundy by which time I was 6 months pregnant. My parents took me to Rosemundy, dad must have made the arrangements. All I knew it was a mother and baby home, you had your baby there and then it was adopted. Miss Launchbury was in charge of the home, a lot of people didn't like her but I found her really nice. Mrs Stait was there and she looked after our welfare. She was lovely. On arrival I was shown where my bed was, 6 of us in a room. There were more than a dozen mothers in the home and we used to all get together to watch the telly in the evenings in the big lounge. Everyone had their morning jobs, we would get up and have breakfast that was ready, and whoever was on breakfast duties would have to get up early to help prepare it. We would then go and do our jobs until lunchtime. The jobs you did each day changed I think every week. There was a laundry room with copper boilers, mangles and large sinks to do all the washing, the stone floors had to be washed. Someone had to help with lunch, do the vegetables, help with the cookery, lay the tables and later wash up. After lunch you were supposed to have a bit of a rest and then you could go out around the village to do a bit of shopping or walk around. The village accepted us, they were quite nice. We all had to go to Church on Sundays. We were well looked after, all the midwives and doctors came in, we were checked for everything.

I was there at Christmas and we had a proper Christmas dinner, we didn't have so many chores to do, some still had to cook and wash up. We had to go to Church; I remember I had a red coat. My baby son was born on the 8th February, there was a proper big delivery room, nurses, midwife and the local doctor came, we were well looked after. If the doctor wasn't there at the time he came soon after. Once the baby was born we went to our own separate rooms for a week, then to a different dormitory with other mothers with babies. We stayed there for 6 weeks.

After about 2 or 3 weeks the people who were going to adopt my son came from Essex to see him. We had to put our babies in nice clothes and go off for the afternoon. I hid and watched to see what they looked like. They were well dressed and very smart. After 6 weeks my mother and father came to take me home and I left my baby there.

I later married another man and had a family with him but always had the idea my baby would come back and find me. He did try to find me; the first two firms who tried to trace me failed, the third lady he contacted wrote to all the houses in the area saying she was looking for me and waited for the letters to come back. A friend of mine who received a letter phoned me and said, 'He's come back, he wants to trace you and he lives in Sweden'. I thought, 'Oh crumbs'. (My husband knew but my children didn't.) I told them and it was fine, my daughter went to meet him and brought him back. He was now called Ian.

DOT

ROSEMUNDY 1962

I came from Somerset to Rosemundy Home, the last week in July 1962 until October 1962. I was 21, afraid and very alone. When I came to the home I was eight and a half months pregnant. I was in a long term relationship when my boyfriend ended it. Sad and very hurt, a one night stand ended with me being pregnant. (No pill or morning-after pill back then.) I didn't tell him or anyone for months, I was in denial and out of my mind with worry and strapping my tummy in so I wouldn't show. But I was losing weight with worry. I was so afraid of my parents I told them I had to go away to work; the firm I worked for was sending me to Plymouth. This was all lies. I went 40 miles away from my home to a lady, Miss Rice, she worked for social services. I told her I was on my own with no parents, she sent me to Rosemundy and I went by train to Truro and by taxi to St Agnes.

I will always remember ringing the doorbell which was answered by a short but large woman, the matron, and I was to learn that she was in charge and that she was to be called matron, I never did know her name. She took me up a grand staircase to a room I shared with 6 other girls. I was never to see the staircase again as we all had to use the back stairs. Life was very hard, we had to scrub the slate floor, the washing was done by hand outside in an old stone building and inside was a brick boiler with a fire underneath which we had to light. (I think it was called a cauldron.) We had to wash dirty nappies, bed linen, sheets from the labour ward and the staff's washing. We did the ironing with old flat-irons and cleaned rooms etc. If it wasn't done well matron would make us do it all again.

It was a harsh regime. Food was short and we lived mostly on bread and jam. Every Sunday we had to march in line up the hill to church with people staring at us. There was a chapel inside the home which we had to go to every morning at 8am. Matron was a very hard woman and let us all know how wicked she thought us all. No compassion. By the time my son Steven was born, two and a half weeks late, I was out of my mind with worry; the only time I saw a doctor was a week before he was born. I wrote to a friend and said I had a son and where I was. That friend came and took me and my baby home. My mum and dad were shocked to see how thin and ill I looked and sad to think that I went through it on my own, but welcomed us both with open arms.

Two years later I married a wonderful man and with him had a son. He has always treated both sons as his own and never treated them any different. We are very proud of both our sons who have given us great joy and love. I am now the proud grandmother of five children. My son was told he was born at Rosemundy and as a family we have spent holidays in St Agnes. As he grew older I asked him if he wanted to know anything about his biological father; to this he answered, 'I know everything about my dad, he's here with me now' (meaning my husband) 'and that is how it will always be'. My husband and I have stayed at Rosemundy, which is now a hotel; nothing is the same, only the grand staircase and the front door which I remember so well. I was the lucky one with a wonderful family and blessed with a good husband. Every night, after 50 years, I still say a prayer for all the girls that ever had to go to the Rosemundy Home and hope somehow they have found peace of mind. Although I kept my baby it lives with you always, and hurt and pain of that goes deep.

Baby Steven.

HELEN

ROSEMUNDY 1964

I arrived there at six months pregnant with no idea what to expect, but it didn't take long to settle in, and, if I'm honest it was really reassuring to be with others in the same predicament! I think there were about a dozen of us there then and we all got on really well although all had different backgrounds. We were made to work hard – laundry, kitchen duties, floor scrubbing – all as well documented, but I don't think we minded too much – it helped to pass the weeks and stopped us dwelling too much on our future.

It wasn't all work and I remember some lovely walks to Trevaunance – easy on the way down but a struggle back up the hill the more one's pregnancy progressed! Evenings were fun too when we all sat with our knitting and watched the new Coronation Street.

The worst days were when a baby left with adoptive parents and we all felt so sad for the "mum" left behind knowing that our turn was not far away. The staff when I was there were basically fair, and as long as we kept to the rules and the daily routine we didn't see a lot of them – maybe the imminent closure of the home had a lot to do with this. I certainly don't recall any lectures on my "sins" although we were made to attend church every Sunday. My actual birth was terrifying because after thirty plus hours in labour I was sent to bed after a third dose of castor oil and told to ring the bell when I started pushing! This I duly did about five hours later only to be told I was "nowhere near" and to get on with it! Twenty minutes later the midwife just got to the end of the bed in time to catch my son!

My story then is more unusual than most because I actually took my baby home. My mother was willing for me to keep him but my grandparents had other ideas and he was finally adopted in October 1964 after being with me for almost five months! This, of course, was devastating, particularly as the adoptive parents came to our house to take him away!

I have traced my son through Norcap who contacted the adoptive parents, and they said he didn't want any contact with me, but I haven't given up.

BABIES

JOHN

BORN 1934

John was born at Rosemundy House on the 22nd May 1934. His mother, Stella, left school before her 15th birthday and went to work at the Kenneggy Hotel near Penzance. When just 14 she became pregnant and was sent to Rosemundy House. The father of the baby was Greek and also worked at the hotel but shot back to Greece when he found out. Stella was not allowed to take the baby home to her parents' house. Her father said, 'No bastard child in this house'. Rosemundy kept John and hoped the situation might change at home. Stella was allowed regular access at Rosemundy and took John out in the pram around St Agnes or sometimes travelled miles on the bus, but had to be back at a certain time each evening. By Christmas 1935 John had been at the Home for over 18 months. One day Stella had John for a visit and took him to Penzance, where she met a sailor who wanted to take her to a dance. She wrapped John up and left him on the steps of Gulval Church while she went off. A man coming home from the pub found John crying, and the police were informed. John had pneumonia and was taken back to Rosemundy, where he nearly died. On Christmas Eve 1935 he was taken by Miss Bence, a foster official, to Dora and John Paddy, foster parents in Truro. Prior to arriving he had had a rubber hot water bottle put on him at Rosemundy, which had caused bad burns and scalds. This disturbed Dora. Staff from Rosemundy would pay regular visits to the house to see John. On the 1st January 1936 Dora gave birth to a son, Neville, and John and Neville grew up as brothers, one dark-haired and one fair. Dora and John fostered many children and also looked after evacuee children during the War, at which time John and Neville slept in a Morrison air-raid shelter in the kitchen. Dora and John Paddy fostered John for eight years. During this period Stella was barred from seeing him or having any contact, but she would hide away or appear on buses to look at him. Sometimes Dora would turn a blind eye and let Stella talk to him. Around this time there was talk of John being adopted by the Paddys but it never happened. When Stella was 21 she went with her father to see a London lawyer and claimed John back. As John was still being fostered and had never been adopted Stella gained custody. John's grandfather and officials from London with a court order came to remove him from his home in Hendra Vean, Truro, and took him away screaming in a car. Stella went to live in London and, it appears, almost immediately put John into a Fegan's Children's Home in Yardley Gobion, near Stony Stratford. Dora and John Paddy were now refused any contact with their foster son and had no idea this had happened. Dora died in 1952, aged just 51. Neville was 16, and shortly before his mother's death she said to him, 'You should try and find out what happened to John, you were very close as boys'. In 1990, with the help of the Salvation Army, Neville found out that John had been sent almost immediately to the Home. Neville received a letter from Fegan's, which informed him that John was admitted to the Home on the 9th July 1942. Yardley Gobion was fairly small and catered for 'little boys' before they moved on to the main orphanage at Stony Stratford itself. He was described as 'a very likeable little chap'. During his time there Stella did not visit and took no interest in him at all. When older, John worked on the Home's farm before leaving to join the Army, but he was soon discharged with heart trouble. Fegan's tried to keep him on their farm at Buxted Park but he found the work too hard. His condition steadily worsened and he was taken to Princess Alice Hospital at Eastbourne. He died there on the 29th July 1953, aged just 19. John was buried in the little churchyard of Buxted Park Church. The work stopped on the farm and the children from the three Fegan's Homes were brought by bus to attend the funeral. The coffin was covered by wreaths from the boys and staff of the three Homes, and there was also a wreath from the farmer and his wife who employed John prior to his illness. Their letter said that they were 'much devoted to him'.

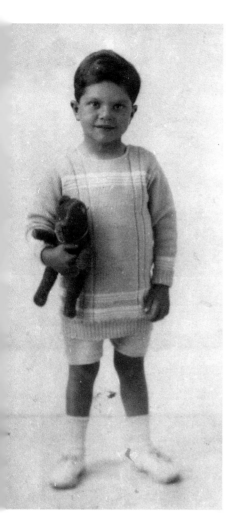

John.

John, Dora and Neville.

PETE

BORN 1937

My mother was 15 when she became pregnant with me and was sent to Rosemundy House for my birth. She was 16 when I was born on the 3rd July 1937. I am not sure how long I was at the Home but a picture I have, taken on the day I left, suggests that I was about one. My mother and I were collected from the Home by my grandmother and my uncle. We went to my grandparents' house at Lelant.

At the age of two I was adopted by a couple in their early forties from Newquay. I assume my mother was too young to keep me, and my grandparents already had four children. It would appear that my mother and grandparents visited the people that adopted me on at least one occasion, and I have photographs of them all together at Newquay. This appears to be during the adoption period and possibly because it was my second birthday. Contact ceased after this and I was brought up by a loving family with their natural son.

My parents never told me I was adopted and I didn't know until I was 21 when I was going for military service, and looking through some family documents I found my adoption papers. I never told my parents that I had found these papers.

Over the years I have found members of my birth mother's family but my mother never wanted to see me. Sadly she has now passed away and the questions I have will never be answered.

Pete at Rosemundy House.

PHIL

BORN 1953

We sped between the hedgerows, past old, isolated bungalows and cottages interspersed with green pastures. As we neared the coastline, the density of the housing increased. Eventually we came to a narrow street which then lurched downwards towards the sea; but the buildings petered out, indicating that we had just passed through what appeared to be the village centre. (St Agnes is actually an agglomerate of five hamlets.)

I was stepping into St Agnes for the first time since my birth. If my mother had arrived with her hopes cheered by the spring of 1953, I entered the village with a chilling sense of foreboding. Until that moment, I had been en route for an afternoon's work of interviewing and filming for our BBC documentary, 'The Crying Shame' (2012). I was focussed on going over my lines for pieces to camera and assembling my story. Yet, suddenly I was in a different space, about to be confronted by a part of "My Life I Never Knew" for the first time. For 46 years, the circumstances of my early childhood and why I was left alone in care, and never knew, heard from or saw my parents or any other relatives, were a haze to me. I had some stories from my godmothers who had known my late mother, but their stories never quite seemed to fit. In 1999, when I had written an article for the *Guardian*, entitled 'My Life I Never Knew', it had concerned my finally gaining access to files which contained reports and letters regarding my birth, abandonment and care – the secrets of my childhood.

I had written: "Now I'm apprehensive. I thought I could be dispassionate about my inquiries. My childhood story concerned people long since out of my life and their human frailties. I was compassionate enough to handle that. So I thought. Instead I'm facing a trip into a labyrinth of undiscovered emotions. It's my emotions that concern me most. What angst stalks in those recesses? What anger, sadness and despair? I'm 45 years old and now I face this journey through the dark. It's a journey I have to take to fill those gaps, to answer why and how."

I sat in the car peering out at the bleak St Agnes scene and, without connecting to those feelings 15 years ago, was overcome by a totally unexpected sense of entering a new darkness full of apprehension. It was more a surprise because, having carried out my research, I hadn't travelled to St Agnes anticipating any new information about my childhood. I was there to report rather than to investigate. I hadn't counted for such emotion.

Perhaps my feelings were brought on by my first ever visit to the place of my primordial existence. I was, after all, entering a part of my life of which I had no conscious memory. Was this my emotional memory asserting itself, emerging from half a century of sleep? Were there emotions and recollections awakening that had been left behind in that village and dormant for decades? They acknowledged my return, but how was I to respond?

There again, perhaps I was picking up not my emotions but the weeping and despair of all those "fallen angels" and Rosemundy babies wrenched from their mothers' final embraces. Was I to them a prodigal son or an adventurer? Whichever way I was in uncharted waters, which carried strange species of sensations shrouded by a mist, which I had no idea how to penetrate. I was, without warning, stripped of being a reporter and left impotent to be thrust tumbling along a passage of discovery. Like Dickens's Scrooge drawn by the Ghost of Christmas Past, I was about to investigate myself.

We eventually reached Rosemundy, where I began life and where my mother, Mavis Frampton, took refuge during the latter part of her pregnancy. Miss Frampton at the time was a music teacher in a Birmingham grammar school. Had the authorities known she was pregnant out of wedlock she would have certainly not been allowed to teach in schools for many years. She was advised to give birth to me as far away as possible from the city and then to leave me in care until she had sorted out her affair with my Nigerian father. However, Mavis's mother, having got wind of her daughter's affair with a Black man, wrote to the Home Office and the Colonial Office, and he, despite being a Nigerian prince, was sent back to Nigeria, just before Mavis became aware that she was pregnant.

The two never did get together again, so, six weeks after I was born, Mavis went back to teaching and I was left at Rosemundy, 250 miles away from her.

Barnardo's had agreed to take me into their care, but didn't have any vacancies. The Moral Welfare Society in Cornwall tried to have me fostered out but quickly declared that there was no chance of a Black child being taken in by a family in the region. After three months, Barnardo's found me a temporary placement with the Invalid Children's Aid Association at Tapeley House near Instow in north Devon. I spent three months in that grand mansion. My mother wrote to say that she wanted me nearer to her so she could visit and I was found a place in a Barnardo's nursery home near Shrewsbury and around 40 miles away from Birmingham.

My mother stopped visiting me after one year. She had fallen in love with a Norwegian student and intended to marry him. However, she wrote to Barnardo's saying that he was jealous of me, the one year old child, and hence

Phil with his mother at Rosemundy House.

she could have no more to do with me. Visits stopped before I was two, so I grew up with no conscious memory of her. I was then considered for adoption but the Matron of the Barnardo's Home wrote that I was "a poor specimen of humanity and there are doubts about his intelligence."

I was four when I was fostered out to a vicar and his wife in Bolton, Lancashire. I was still four when they handed me back, the wife declaring that I woke up too early, talked too much and was a bad influence on her nine year old son. This time I was sent to a ramshackle Barnardo's home, housing 40 children in Southport, Liverpool's seaside resort. After two years I was moved to another large Southport home. I was 15 when an abusive ex-army officer took charge of the home. I was desperate to move into digs and live on my own. Eventually he got me fostered out to an abusive middle class couple in the town, so I hardly lasted a year. At 16, I finally got a place in a dingy bedsit on my own. It was situated near the town station and populated by down and outs but it would be my home whilst I studied at school for my A Levels.

I had finished my A Levels and was still 17 when I was allowed to leave school early because I would soon be out of care and with nowhere to live. I had applied for and was offered a live-in job in Cornwall at Mullion Cove Hotel, not far from St Agnes. I never visited my birthplace. At the hotel, I learned that my A Level results would allow me to go to Bristol University, so I ended up living in the South West for seven years. I often visited Mullion but never St Agnes. I was too busy sorting out my life ... and the rest of the world.

PHIL FRAMPTON

Author, *The Golly in the Cupboard*
www.philframpton.co.uk

PETER

BORN 1956

I was born there in January 1956 as Philip and adopted later the same year. My adoptive parents were fantastic and I thank God for their love and kindness. They always let me know I was adopted and eventually when I was a teenager I was told what my original birth name was; I will always remember that seminal moment. I was always interested in history at school and in my late teens (1972) I became interested in family history and so traced my adoptive family tree with the help of my adoptive parents, grandparents and relatives; they must have seen my genealogical interest differently to me, but at that time my adoption didn't really loom large in my consciousness. After a while it dawned on me that I also had another family somewhere and I naturally tried to trace my biological mother's family in 1974, but I was too young to really make much progress. I always maintained my interest in genealogy and this was the driver for me to have another go at tracing my biological ancestry when I had the opportunity in my mid twenties. I had been working in Saudi Arabia and finally had enough of the heat and tough life and decided to spend a year at home in North Devon; I used my long holiday of over a year to continue my research into my ancestry and resolved to be very pro-active in tracing my biological mother. I thought it was a now or never time in my life and luckily I achieved my goal in finding a lady at Lanhydrock who knew my mother (and my presumed biological father). I have been very meticulous in my record keeping so I have all the evidence of my genealogical journey.

I can let you know that after a few years I eventually contacted my birth mother, who was Dutch, and she confirmed my suspicions over the identity of my father, and I was able to research my biological family tree in great detail, which was my goal. Several years later I met my mother who now lives in Canada and had a happy reunion. When her parents in the Netherlands had both died she felt able to tell her own daughter and siblings about me and now I have regular contact with them. My father who was also Dutch never acknowledged me, although I did continue to write to him on many occasions. After he died in 1990, his children found some of my correspondence tucked away inside his stamp collection and from that evidence they made contact with me; so I had a happy reunion with my father's side of the family also, and eventually with all my aunts, uncles, and cousins. My mother went to the Home about five months before I was born (circa September 1955) and had a relatively good time at Rosemundy as she was given special treatment by a Miss Jones, who was a friend of Miss Ackroyd, the director of Rosemundy House. My mother was excused laundry duty whilst in the home and spent some of her time cleaning Miss Ackroyd's cottage to keep her away from some of the rougher women that were in the home. She remembered having to walk to church on Sundays and feeling embarrassed to walk past the congregation to sit on the pews at the back of the church for the service. After she was discharged from the Home my mother was helped to obtain work as a nurse's aid at St. Austell Hospital by Miss Ackroyd, and I have some of the letters my mother wrote to her as they were kept in my adoption file. So thank you Miss Ackroyd for aiding my mother into the noble career of nursing.

Peter with midwife Nurse Waite.

OPEN-AIR THEATRE

On the 8th July 1954 an open-air theatre was inaugurated in the grounds of Rosemundy House. The grounds had been used for many village activities and it was that fact that inspired the idea of an outdoor stage and theatre that could be used for the benefit of the community. The work was planned by a small committee and carried out largely by local effort. It would provide hundreds of people with an equally good view of the stage with excellent acoustic quality. The theatre was opened and dedicated by the Bishop of Truro (the Rt Revd E.R. Morgan) assisted by the Revd Clifford Lever, Superintendent Minister of St Mary's Methodist Circuit, Truro, as a memorial to Miss Margaret Smith of Truro, for many years Secretary of the Cornwall Social and Moral Welfare Association, and also in honour of Miss Barbara Ackroyd, Matron of Rosemundy Home. Three slabs built into the lower wall of the theatre, one commemorating the date of its opening and dedication, and two others bearing the name of Miss Smith and Miss Ackroyd, were unveiled by three pupils of schools in Truro of which Miss Smith was a governor. Mr Jack Simmons, chairman of St Agnes Parish Council, welcomed a large gathering, which included members of the Parish Council, Cornwall Social and Moral Welfare Association and Friends of Rosemundy, together with the vicar of St Agnes, the Revd G.H. Barnicoat.

He said the committee of the Garden Theatre had asked him to impress upon residents that they must consider it a part of the town's communal life, and not merely a private theatre for functions associated with Rosemundy House. Following the opening, Cornwall Religious Drama Group presented 'Thor with Angels' in the new theatre.

On the 17th March 1955 the Rosemundy Garden Theatre Players were formed, and in 1956 they put on their first performance in the new theatre, 'Toad Of Toad Hall'. This was followed by productions every year until 1967:

1957   A Midsummer Night's Dream

1958   Twelfth Night

1959   The Farmer's Wife

1960   Thieves' Carnival

1961   A Hundred Years Old

1962   The Noble Spaniard

1963   Dear Brutus

1964   The Lady's Not For Burning

In 1964 Rosemundy House closed and was locked and secured. Plays however continued:

1965   The Devil's Disciple

1966   The Nightingale

By 1966 the House had been closed and boarded up for a couple of years, but the Charity Commissioners had now given their consent to sell it. The following appeared in the programme for 'The Nightingale' under 'Future of this theatre':

> Many of our audiences will no doubt be aware that Rosemundy House and grounds are soon to be sold on the open market. This could of course mean the end of this beautiful theatre. We sincerely hope, however, that whoever buys the property will value the theatre and preserve it – not only for the use of the Garden Theatre Players but possibly for other visiting Companies. Indeed, if we were in a financial position to do so, we should ourselves like to own the property and make Rosemundy into a permanent open theatre. We welcome your views and suggestions. We hope and believe that those of you who have supported our productions over the past ten years have had pleasure from the theatre. Although we have no new 'Home' in mind should our present abode be denied us, we are determined to "stay in business" - Show Business!

The final play at Rosemundy House was:

1967   Ring Round the Moon

In late 1967 Rosemundy House was reopened as a hotel. The new owner Derek Tabor was very supportive of the players and gave them permission to continue performing in the grounds. He realised they were handicapped because of the lack of amenities and said he would install permanent electrical facilities for them. In 1968 they started rehearsing at Rosemundy for their summer production 'The Tempest' but found it very difficult; with Rosemundy House now a hotel there was a large increase in the number of cars coming and going, and rehearsing was almost impossible because of the noise. Sadly a new location had to be found and the production was moved to the gardens of a large house at Wheal Butson, St Agnes. The following year the players moved indoors to the Church Hall and adopted the new name of St Agnes Theatre Players.

The opening of the theatre by the Bishop of Truro.

bove: Theatre in 1954. *Below:* The production of 'The Farmer's Wife' in 1959.

FLORA DANCES

The Flora Dance in St Agnes started in 1948 when the Tennis Club were looking for a way to raise money for new courts in Goonvrea Road, the cost of each court being £1000. Music was needed and they asked St Agnes Silver Band to join in. At first the dancers were only from the Tennis Club and, led by the band, they would dance through the village to Peterville and finish in the grounds of Rosemundy House. Here the spectators would gather to listen to the band and watch the choosing of the Carnival Queen and the Fairy Queen.

Various stalls providing food, drink and games raised money which was used by the Tennis Club for their courts and by the band to renovate the band room.

By the 1960s the Tennis Club dancers were replaced by local schoolchildren, and the tradition continues today with two dances every year, performed by St Agnes, Mithian, Mount Hawke and Blackwater Schools.

In June 2008 two Flora Dances were held to mark the 60th anniversary. To celebrate this, the dancers were led by members of today's Tennis Club.

ove: Dancers outside Rosemundy House 1964. *Below:* Dancers at Rosemundy House 2008, led by members of St
nes Tennis Club.

HOME TO HOTEL

Following its closure in October 1964 Rosemundy House remained empty for three years. On the 11th November 1965, under the heading 'Rosemundy House to be sold', the *West Briton* reported:

Rosemundy the former home for unmarried mothers in St Agnes is to be sold. The decision after months of speculation about its future was announced by the home's owners Cornwall Social and Moral Welfare Association. The association had obtained consent from the charity commissioners as the facilities formerly available at Rosemundy are now provided by the County Council. A report to Truro Rural District Council by Mr H.P. Dorey, the clerk, said it was a legal requirement that the property should be sold at the best possible price.

In December 1965 seven St Agnes residents formed a group called 'The St Agnes Community Trust'. A document held at St Agnes Museum states that the aim of the group was to purchase Rosemundy House so that it could be used for three main purposes:

1. As a **Community Centre**, with facilities for parishioners of all ages.

2. As an **Arts Centre**, for all the varied interests in this talented community.

3. As a **Festival Centre**: a centre for music, drama, ballet, opera, painting, crafts and so forth, varied to suit different tastes.

The document continues:

> Please remember that the St Agnes Community Trust can come to birth and be effectual only if it attracts very wide support. Its success or failure will depend on YOU.

We do not know how much support 'The St Agnes Community Trust' received during the following year but in December 1966 it had a new name, 'The Rosemundy Project', and if Rosemundy House were purchased, it would become 'The Rosemundy Nature Trust'. It was hoped that a 'Lady Private Donor' (or a group of ladies) would be found, who would gladly provide necessary funds to acquire the estate. The Trust also had new aims:

1. To provide a Centre in Cornwall for the co-ordination of all efforts to reconcile Man with his Natural Enviroment, in all of its infinite manifestations.

2. To function as a modest 'mini' or 'micro' University of Natural History and Science, with courses to be held, under the tuition of fully qualified resident directors and assistants, in Zoology, Botany, Biology, Geology, Ecology and so forth, covering all aspects of the Natural Sciences.

3. To operate a Field Training Centre, later with Outward Bound type character-training schools as satellites, with accommodation at Rosemundy for a minimum of fifty students at one time.

4. To provide safe research facilities, with special emphasis upon the sublittoral aspects of Marine Biology. For this purpose a South Cornwall satellite laboratory will be sought in due course, equipped with a converted trailer for sub-aqua operations.

Further proposals are put forward:

> The four acres, more or less, of beautiful, sloping and heavily wooded grounds of Rosemundy (at one time in the possession of the renowned Carne Family, whose sons have blazed such a trail of glory in H.M. Forces), which already constitutes a superb natural bird sanctuary, will be preserved and adorned by the construction of pools, cascades and pleasances at virtually no expense, since there already flows through the estate a swift stream of crystal clear water. The public will be admitted to the grounds on payment of a suitable entrance fee, to cover the cost of improvement and maintenance and also to populate the sanctuary with other birds and animal life, for their own joy and our instruction. There is no doubt it will prove popular among visitors and children of all ages. It is, of course, directly inspired by the pioneer work of Peter Scott, to whom we all owe so much ... The existing open-air stage, dedicated by the Lord Bishop of Truro in 1954 and situate across the greensward which fronts the house itself, will still and most gladly, be made available to the enthusiasts of the St Agnes Garden Theatre Players ... it may become, so to say, a second Minack Theatre ...

In the end the project failed – one can only assume that the Lady Donor and necessary support were not found. It does however make you wonder what Rosemundy House and grounds would be like today if the project had gone ahead.

The house was eventually purchased by Mr Derek Tabor of Truro. He was a principal of the Truro development company of Mitchell-Hill Properties Ltd, who planned to turn it into a hotel with 12 or 14 bedrooms and hoped to add 14 more, each with a private bathroom.

In February 1967 work started on modernising the interior and conversion into a hotel. Derek told the writer:

> I knew nothing – 'I could hardly boil an egg' – but if you make your mind up to do something you can. The place was pretty run down, other than essential necessities; repairs must have been kept to a minimum by the Cornwall County Council. However, the property was of solid construction and waterproof when I bought it. I did a considerable amount of work to make it useable, altering existing bedrooms, lounges, converting storerooms into bedrooms, building a bar in what I call the slate room (before the Tom Noggi room was built), installing fire doors

Above: Rosemundy House converted to a hotel in 1967. *Below left:* Derek Tabor (centre of picture) stands by the side of his newly constructed swimming pool. *Below right:* Derek Tabor in the 1980s.

Rosemundy House Hotel

ST. AGNES, CORNWALL

Delightful Queen Anne residence, recently professionally converted, with all modern amenities and yet retaining its charm, set in three acres of beautiful grounds, quiet and secluded, but yet a short distance to local beaches and ideal for touring Cornwall.

Throughout the summer the centre for the ancient St. Agnes Flora Dances, and regular performances by the Silver Band and Theatre Group in our own outdoor theatre.

17 well furnished bedrooms, all with H. & C., some family suites and a number of bedrooms with private bathrooms.

Cottage available in grounds.

Fully licensed Restaurant with attractive cocktail bar, comfortable lounges and TV room. Games rooms for adults and children.
Our speciality—Good Food and Friendliness.
Open all the year round including Christmas.

Write for our fully illustrated brochure or telephone St. Agnes 317

Advertisement for the newly opened hotel.

to comply with regulations – all being essential before being able to operate as a hotel. In 1968 I built the Tom Noggi room, and to do this I had to blow up the gazebo on the end of the house. This led from upstairs to the ground floor. I secured the help of a dynamite expert (I knew a chap who worked at ECLP with a dynamite certificate), and the thing went bang, strewing the lawn with blocks of concrete and granite. These were so heavy, lorries wouldn't take them because they were worried about damage to their vehicles, so I buried them in the foundations for the restaurant and the lorries took the earth instead. While carrying out this work I found steps beside the house going to a room under the slate room. There was a door leading to a passage under the house which I believe went to the coast and may have been used for smuggling hundreds of years ago. When I had finished building the Tom Noggi restaurant I modernised the kitchens and then added en-suite rooms set back on the upper level above the new restaurant. Additional rooms were added to the left of the hotel on the lower and upper levels. The swimming pool, amenity block and bedrooms overlooking the pool were also added. I created staff quarters at the back of the building in a room where the nappies from the mother and baby home were washed. There were several 2' x 2' basins there which I gave away for horse troughs etc. Above this room in the old flat at the back there were drying rails on pulleys for nappies and other washing to dry.

The hotel opened for guests in the summer of 1967. Derek Tabor remembered that one of his earliest guests was Albert Locke, who produced for the London Palladium and also the Royal Command Performance, to which Derek was invited. Mr Locke returned to stay at the hotel over several years. He was not the only famous person to stay there during Derek's time as proprietor. Between St Agnes and Perranporth, in the village of Trevellas, there was for many years in the 1970s a nightclub called the 'Talk of the West' where, despite its remote location in the depths of Cornwall, many of the great performers of the day appeared and stayed at the Rosemundy House Hotel. Derek Tabor remembered them well:

> Guests staying at the hotel, whilst working at the 'Talk of the West', included Dick Emery, Tommy Cooper, Des O'Connor, Anita Harris, the New Seekers, Marty Wilde and Harry Secombe. Tommy Cooper was a difficult one – the staff were reluctant to take anything to his room! Harry Secombe was a wonderful guest, full of fun and even gave a private rendering of some of his songs to the staff and myself. The New Seekers were a great group which included Eve Graham and Lyn Paul who later went solo. I recall on one occasion the 'Talk of the West' giving Lyn Paul a birthday party to which I was invited, much to my embarrassment, for they had gone to a lot of trouble with snacks etc. In the midst of it all, Lyn Paul announced that she wanted to return 'Now! Now!' to Rosemundy ... We returned to the hotel, opened up the bar and the party celebrations continued until the early hours. Luckily, at the time no other guests were staying at the hotel!

Derek sold the hotel in 1982. He said:

> Some of the happiest years of my life were spent creating Rosemundy House into a hotel, and it was always a challenge to make people enjoy their stay there. Local people like Trevor and Chris Hodge, Malcolm Carveth, Phyllis and Arthur Robinson, Sid Rosevear, Chris and Margaret Williams, Henry Gilbert and his wife and many others, were all wonderful people who all played a part in making Rosemundy House so successful.

In 1982 the hotel was sold to Steve and Veronica Manico, who ran it until 1999, when the building was sold to its current owners, Derek and Marion Faulkner. The couple had previously run hotels in Newquay. Derek and Marion, together with sons Kevin and Martin, have spent a considerable amount of time, money and effort in getting the hotel up to scratch to meet the needs of visitors today, including menus that are all three-star AA standard, which was achieved in June 2006. Derek said: 'A few guests have let us know that they were born at the hotel when it was the Mother and Baby Home. Although it has changed considerably since then, it still has a resonance in those people's lives.'

Marion and Derek Faulkner with Derek Tabor when he stayed at the hotel in 2009.

REFERENCES

The Carne Collection, Courtney Library, Royal Institution of Cornwall, Truro

Friendly Retreat by Maurice Bizley

Royal Cornwall Gazette (Cornwall Centre, Redruth)

West Briton (Cornwall Centre, Redruth)

Old Falmouth by S.E. Gay

The Cornish Riviera by the Great Western Railway Company

Sale of Rosemundy House agreement, 1919 (Cornwall Record Office, Truro)

Cornwall Preventive and Rescue Association annual reports, 1919-1942 (Cornwall Record Office, Truro)

Cornwall Social and Moral Welfare Association annual reports, 1942-1963 (Cornwall Record Office Truro)

Gwendroc Paper, Number 11. Moral Welfare Work in Cornwall (Courtney Library, Royal Institution of Cornwall, Truro)

An Account of St Agnes Life, 1822 to 1908 by Isaac Rowse (St Agnes Museum)

The History of Cornwall from the Earliest Records and Traditions to the Present Time (1824).

Books by the same author:

St Agnes Parish 1850-1920: a Photographic Record (1986)

St Agnes Parish 1920-1950: a Photographic Record (1988)

Around St Agnes – The Archive Photographs series (1996)

St Agnes: a Photographic History. Volume One – Down Quay (2005)

St Agnes: a Photographic History. Volume Two – Village & Shops (2006)

St Agnes: a Photographic History. Volume Three – Down to Dirty Pool (2009)

St Agnes: a Photographic History. Volume Four – Up Goonown & Goonbell (2012)

Books by the same author with Tony Mansell:

A History of Blackwater and its Neighbours (2004)

Jericho to Cligga, Trevellas & Crosscoombe (2006)

Our Village Church, St Agnes, Cornwall (2007)

Memories of Mount Hawke (2008)

I rode to St Agnes: John Wesley and Methodism in a Cornish Parish (2010)

ACKNOWLEDGEMENTS

Once again during the research for a book, people have been only too pleased to help me with information and photographs.

The book is actually made up of three parts: The Family Home, The Mother and Baby Home, and the Hotel. Various people have helped me with different sections.

I would like to thank the following for their help with the pre-1919 period:

Tim Adkin, Sarah Bott, Francis Carne, David Chilcott, Diana Hitchcock and Belle Hollingsworth.

It is somewhat more difficult to publicly thank everyone who helped me with the second section. Many mothers, as well as children born at the Home, have written to me but wish to remain anonymous. Some of their stories are recorded in the book with just a Christian name – these people know who they are and I thank them all so much for taking the time to contact me and tell me about their time at Rosemundy. I sincerely hope that some enjoyment and peace will come from this book for all of you.

I would also like to thank the following:

Margaret Howlett (née Smith) (Nurse, Rosemundy 1951-1959), Joe Ridholls (St Agnes Methodist Minister, 1957-1962) and Neville Paddy.

For the final section of the book I would like to thank the following:

Derek and Deborah Tabor, Derek and Marion Faulkner, Peter Hayes, Sharon Mula.

Once again my research has been helped by the staff of the Courtney Library at the Royal Institution of Cornwall, the Cornwall Centre and the Cornwall Record Office. These are invaluable sources of information for local historians.

Finally I would like to thank Peter ('Nick') Thomas for his time in proofreading the completed book and my son Daniel for his design and typesetting skills.

Rosemundy House today.